Peers, Pirates, and Persuasion

Peers, Pirates, and Persuasion

Rhetoric in the Peer-to-Peer Debates

John Logie

Parlor Press
West Lafayette, Indiana
www.parlorpress.com

Parlor Press LLC, 816 Robinson Street, West Lafayette, Indiana 47906

This work is licensed under the Creative Commons Attribution-NonCommercial-NoDerivs 2.5 License, with no prejudice to any material quoted from *Peers, Pirates, and Persuasion: Rhetoric in the Peer-to-Peer Debates* or other texts under fair use principles. To view a copy of this license, visit http://creativecommons.org/licenses/by-nc-nd/2.5/ or send a letter to Creative Commons, 543 Howard Street, 5th Floor, San Francisco, California, 94105, USA.

© 2006 by Parlor Press
All rights reserved.
Printed in the United States of America
S A N: 2 5 4 – 8 8 7 9

Library of Congress Cataloging-in-Publication Data

Logie, John.
  Peers, pirates, and persuasion : rhetoric in the peer-to-peer debates / John Logie.
      p. cm.
  Includes bibliographical references and index.
  ISBN 978-1-60235-005-2 (pbk. : alk. paper) -- ISBN 978-1-60235-006-9 (Adobe ebook)
  1. Sound recordings--Pirated editions--United States. 2. Music trade--Law and legislation--United States. 3. Peer-to-peer architecture (Computer networks)--Law and legislation--United States. 4. Downloading of data--Law and legislation--United States. I. Title.
  KF3045.4.L64 2006
  346.7304'82--dc22
                              2006103287

Cover and book design by David Blakesley
"Digital Audio" © by Ben Goode. Used by permission.
"Skull and Cross Bones" © by Lewis Wright. Used by permission.
Printed on acid-free paper.

Parlor Press, LLC is an independent publisher of scholarly and trade titles in print and multimedia formats. This book is available in paperback, cloth, and Adobe eBook formats from Parlor Press on the Internet at http://www.parlorpress.com or through online and brick-and-mortar bookstores. For submission information or to find out about Parlor Press publications, write to Parlor Press, 816 Robinson Street, West Lafayette, Indiana, 47906, or e-mail editor@parlorpress.com.

For my wife, Carol, without whom . . .

Contents

Illustrations	*viii*
Acknowledgments	*ix*
1 Introduction: The Cat Is Out of the Bag	*3*
2 Hackers, Crackers, and the Criminalization of Peer-to-Peer Technologies	*22*
3 The Positioning of Peer-to-Peer Transfers as Theft	*45*
4 Peer-to-Peer Technologies as Piracy	*67*
5 The Problem of "Sharing" in Digital Environments	*85*
6 Peer-to-Peer as Combat	*105*
7 Conclusion: The Cat Came Back	*127*
Appendix: On Images and Permissions	*149*
Works Cited	*152*
Index	*159*

Illustrations

Figure 1.	The Ukrainian Iggy Pop MP3 Collection.	*10*
Figure 2.	Original and revised versions of the Napster logo.	*35*
Figure 3.	An image from Napster's website depicting Shawn Fanning in a dormitory-like setting.	*37*
Figure 4.	Apple's "Rip. Mix. Burn." campaign.	*61*
Figure 5.	A first-generation iPod bearing the "Don't Steal Music" sticker.	*62*
Figure 6.	Cake songs available via the Limewire peer-to-peer client.	*87*
Figure 7.	The EFF's campaign in support of "File-Sharing."	*101*
Figure 8.	The logo for an anti-RIAA site; note the use of "Live Free or Die!"	*110*
Figure 9:	The "Kill the RIAA" Protocol.	*111*
Figure 10:	The warning posted by the MPAA to the former LokiTorrent site.	*124*
Figure 11:	The ShutdownThis.com "Army of Mice" parody.	*125*

Acknowledgments

Scholars whose research addresses the field now referred to as "intellectual property" usually conclude that writing is by no means a solitary pursuit. In my case, this is especially true. As I complete this project, I am keenly conscious that I will not be able to offer a truly *complete* list of those who helped influence my thinking, productively challenged my arguments, or supported me in other ways as this project unfolded.

First I must thank my colleagues in the University of Minnesota's Department of Rhetoric, especially Art Walzer and Alan Gross who were both kind enough to read and comment on early drafts of this project. I am also grateful to Vickie Mikelonis for organizing the trip to Ukraine that so powerfully illustrated that the U.S.'s approach to copyright was—to put it mildly—*highly* context-specific. I have also benefited from my work with my department's exceptional graduate students, many of whom have prompted me to revisit and revise some of my most-favored arguments. Five particularly deserving of my thanks are Laurie Johnson, Krista Kennedy, Clancy Ratliff, Jessica Reyman, and Jeff Ward.

Lawrence Lessig and Siva Vaidhyanathan were both kind enough to meet with students in my graduate seminars. Both have also offered supportive comments as this project unfolded and, in general, demonstrated the collegial generosity that is especially common among scholars pursuing a critical reading of contemporary copyright.

I am also especially grateful to Andrea Lunsford and Jim Porter, both of whom have, for many years, served as leaders in scholarship addressing the intersections of composition and copyright. Andrea and Jim have always been generous with their time, and have on numerous occasions helped me to take important steps in my own development as a scholar. It was Andrea and Jim's active, engaged leadership that attracted me to the Intellectual Property Caucus of the Conference on

College Composition and Communication (CCCC-IP). This organization has consistently offered a rich site for engaged scholars to meet and discuss the implications of our ever-changing intellectual property laws for teachers of writing and rhetoric.

The University of Minnesota deserves my thanks for the Faculty Summer Research Fellowship that funded a critical period in my development of this project.

Special thanks go to Charlie Lowe at Parlor Press, whose comments prompted significant improvements in this text. Thanks also to Parlor Press publisher David Blakesley, who is bringing a spirit of adventure back to scholarly publishing.

Thanks also to Mike Cohen for having had the presence of mind to photograph the sticker on his first-generation iPod before unwrapping it. And thanks to the editors of both *First Monday* and "The International Handbook of Virtual Learning Environments" for publishing earlier versions of some of the material found herein.

But above all, I wish to thank my family. My immediate family—my wife Carol, and my daughters, Nora and Shane—deserve special acknowledgment for having put up with my diminished availability as I pursued the final stages of my first draft. I am immensely appreciative for their gifts of time and space to pursue this project. My parents, siblings, and in-laws have also been supportive and understanding as I pressed toward publication.

Finally, I am grateful to the musicians whose work I listened to as I wrote. I hope this work helps fuel a move toward Internet-based music distribution that fairly and fully compensates you for your tremendous contributions to our culture.

Peers, Pirates, and Persuasion

When a new technology strikes a society, the most natural reaction is to clutch at the immediately preceding period for familiar and comforting images. . . . What is called progress and advanced thinking is nearly always of the rear-view mirror variety.

—Marshall McLuhan and Quentin Fiore,
The Medium is the Massage

1 Introduction

The Cat Is Out of the Bag

In the Spring of 2000 I was completing a shopping trip to Costco, a "warehouse club" located in a Minneapolis suburb, when I got an unexpected lesson in the burgeoning popularity of Napster, the peer-to-peer file-transfer program developed by Shawn Fanning in 1998. Costco makes a practice of having employees "check off" the merchandise on your receipt as an anti-theft measure, so the checker is effectively reviewing your purchases one by one. The roughly sixty-year-old man who was checking my receipt noticed I had purchased a CD labeling kit. His face brightened.

"Hey, you use Napster?" he asked.

"Sometimes," I responded, warily.

"Isn't it the greatest?" he exclaimed. "I've been getting all the songs on my old records that they won't put out on CD. I make my own mixes!"

He went on to sing the praises of Napster, which was offering him and like-minded sexagenarians on opportunity to exchange their favorite music—mostly obscure album tracks by Bert Kaempfert and Herb Alpert and the Tijuana Brass, as near as I could tell—and recommended the service to me as a source for such lost gems.

"Aren't you worried about copyright?" I asked.

"I bought all these records back in the sixties," he answered, "and if they reissue them on CD, I might buy them again. But right now I can't get this stuff on CD. I know a bunch of people through Napster who are trading this music. Maybe the record labels will see how many of us like this stuff and get going on it."

To this point my own image of the stereotypical Napster user was epitomized by the self-presentation of Napster's founder, Shawn Fanning, who maintained his ballcap-wearing, dorm rat persona well beyond the end of his career as a Northeastern University student. I also knew many of my own students were fans of Napster. Because my academic department has a strong undergraduate program in scientific and technical communication, my technologically inclined students are often early adopters of new technologies of all kinds. I had discussed Napster with some of them, and as a voracious consumer of popular music, I understood their enthusiasm for the kinds of discoveries Napster enabled.

But here, in his Costco vest, was another kind of Napster user, and one who was not simply using the software, but proselytizing for it. When I mentioned copyright as a concern, he had a ready defense. Indeed, he went as far as suggesting that his use of Napster was alerting a somnambulant music industry to the presence of a demand that they were not adequately addressing. Thus, to his way of thinking (or at least within his rationalization) Napster was *helping* record labels understand consumer demand.

While this gentleman may or may not have been absolutely clear on the dicey status of his actions with respect to U.S. copyright laws, he was clearly aware that Napster's content was getting better and better as more and more people logged on. And even if I didn't share his love for the Tijuana Brass, he understood that increasing the number of participants on Napster meant an increased likelihood of finding an obscure song via the service. For a brief moment, Napster users had a glimpse of the kind of expansive electronic library that copyright laws typically preclude . . . everything in no particular order, all day, all night, and in stereo. This from a service that had popped onto the U.S. public's radar screen in March of 1999, mere months before my trip to Costco.

It is at times difficult to recall an Internet predating the peer-to-peer networking that is now so commonplace, but Napster, the program that popularized peer-to-peer exchanges, arrived fairly late in the life of the Internet—a full decade after the development of the http protocol that underpins the World Wide Web. Napster incorporated in May of 1999. The company's website "went live" in August of that year, offering an elegant user interface for locating and downloading music files compressed in the MP3 format via the Internet. As word spread among savvy Internet users Napster's network experienced exponential growth. Napster's users began transferring not only current popular music, but also arcane, hard-to-find, and out-of-print music.

Within weeks of Napster's launch, the traffic to and from Napster's servers was becoming a significant problem for network administrators at universities across the U.S. Recognizing the significant likelihood that much of this traffic was enabling infringements of copyright, the Recording Industry Association of America filed suit against Napster in December of 1999. In January of 2000, after discovering that somewhere between 20 to 30 percent of *all* the traffic on its servers was Napster-directed, Northwestern University blocked student access to Napster on its networks (Gold). In April of 2000, the hard rock band Metallica, and hip-hop producer and performer Dr. Dre also sued Napster, alleging copyright infringement and racketeering (Borland). Napster, in the wake of the publicity afforded by these high-profile lawsuits, became far and away the most popular file-transfer service on the Internet. This prompted an additional wave of legal go-rounds and injunctions, ultimately resulting in the demise of Napster as a free peer-to-peer network, when its servers were shut down in July of 2001.

At its peak, Napster is estimated to have had more than 80 million registered users. In just the month of February of 2001, the best estimates suggest that 2.8 *billion* files were transferred over the network Napster facilitated (Kornblum). Because the Internet is international in its scope and reach, it is impossible to determine what percentage of these transfers were made by United States-based users, but given the general distribution of computer technology worldwide, it is almost certain that the vast majority of Napster's users hailed from the U.S. And this use of Napster was transpiring despite the users' awareness that the technology at the heart of Napster's network was based on a questionable interpretation of U.S. copyright laws. In fact, Napster users' knowledge of the possibility that a July 29, 2000 injunction could shut down Napster's servers prompted a flurry of downloading in the few days before the injunction was to take effect (Konrad, "Napster Fans"). The dramatic spike in downloads suggests that Napster fans were actively indulging in a "last call" in anticipation of the court ruling Napster to be illegal. When Napster finally did shut down, in 2001, similar services, pursuing a second dot-com bubble, were leaping to fill the void.

In 2006, the number of users of post-Napster peer-to-peer applications including Kazaa, BitTorrent, and various Gnutella clients dwarfed Napster's purported totals. And these users are downloading without evident regard for the lawsuits threatened by the Recording Industry Association of America. Indeed, peer-to-peer users have, by and large, persisted in the same patterns of behavior that they did via Napster, and have even extended their napsterization of cultural artifacts, freely downloading film, video, and photographic files via current peer-to-peer applications. And they are often doing so in defiance of the law as it is commonly (mis)understood.

Organizations representing the corporations and businesses associated with the marketing and sale of creative work, especially music and motion pictures, have argued for years that Internet-based transfers of media files threaten their livelihood. The particularly vociferous complaints of film studios, as represented by the Motion Picture Association of America (MPAA) and record companies, as represented by the Recording Industry Association of America (RIAA) have risen steadily as the Internet expanded. In the mid-1990s, as the Internet shifted decisively from its early roots in academia (reflected in the preponderance of "dot edu" domains) to a more commercial orientation ("dot com"), the consistency with which the film and music industry made parallel arguments critiquing Internet practices prompted the coinage of the umbrella term *content industries*, which now functions as a shorthand descriptor for the largest and most powerful media companies. As this book heads to press, the content industries seem to have both won and lost these arguments. Most U.S. residents have been persuaded (in some cases, incorrectly) that peer-to-peer networks trafficking in copyrighted materials are violating the law. That said, many people continue to download copyrighted materials in spite of their understanding that this activity is quite possibly illegal.

This book will address the content industries' arguments, and the key terms and metaphors underpinning their arguments. This book will also interrogate peer-to-peer enthusiasts' various responses to these arguments, and the limited applicability of this community's favored metaphors and models. In particular, I will endeavor to explain how it is that the content industries' efforts have proven demonstrably persuasive in U.S. courts and in the houses of Congress but also have demonstrably *failed* to persuade peer-to-peer enthusiasts to change their behavior. The arguments made throughout the peer-to-peer debates are often striking in and of themselves, but this book will place them in the broader context of how citizens persuade one another on matters of public policy, and the consequences of these persuasive efforts.

My training in rhetorical theory and history offers me considerable support in my efforts to understand the peer-to-peer debates. To my initial surprise, the peer-to-peer debates have been driven chiefly by appeals to emotion and to the personal credibility of the participants—Aristotle's *pathos* and *ethos* appeals, respectively—at the expense of the *logos* appeal. At first blush, the peer-to-peer debate would seem resolvable almost solely through recourse to questions of logic and reason, the kinds of questions historically recognized as the province of *logos*. Indeed, because the peer-to-peer debates ultimately stem from a public policy question, we might anticipate the debate to be characterized by the kinds of persuasive strategies conventionally associated with *logos* appeals. In his treatment of *logos* for the *Encyclopedia of Rhetoric and Composition*, George Yoos offers the following exhaustive list of the *logos* appeal's preferred rhetorical strategies: "premises, warrants, evidence, facts, data, observations, backing, support, explanations, causes, signs, commonplaces, principles, or maxims" (411). Yoos specifies that this list applies only to the disciplines of "oratory and public address, argumentation, and forensics," acknowledging that logical operations outside these fields might take on additional forms. But even this circumscribed list initially seems adequate to the task of unpacking the peer-to-peer debates. Yoos's fourteen favored *logos* strategies appear to encompass the arc of arguments rising from the debate.

But as the peer-to-peer debates unfolded, these persuasive strategies were repeatedly supplanted by arguments grounded in appeals to authority (*ethos*) and emotion (*pathos*). This narrative offers a telling index of the politics of persuasion in the 21st Century. The participants in the peer-to-peer debates have largely abandoned *logos* appeals because these appeals do not resonate with the general public as powerfully as *ethos* and *pathos* appeals.

In my decade as a rhetorician addressing questions of invention, authorship, and copyright, I have often wondered why arguments about copyright generate so much passion. Though most people claim to know little about intellectual property law, many also have extremely strong opinions about their rights and responsibilities as consumers of popular media. Internet discussion groups are filled with individuals raging about digital rights management (DRM) and the decline of the public domain. But the stakes of debates over intellectual property are *never* life-and-death, and recent history is, unfortunately, filled with examples of actual life-and-death arguments. At times, my research on the rhetoric of the peer-to-peer debates seemed trivial when compared with potential work on the rhetoric attendant to war, or debates over the right to abortion, or the right of *habeas corpus,* to highlight just a few examples. And yet I have persisted, because I've come to recognize that in this case my training as a rhetorician meshes with my own history as a music critic, record collector, and exceedingly briefly (and ineptly) as a performing musician. In short, my lifelong connection to popular music intersects with these issues in ways that help me understand the discourse of this debate's participants. And while the stakes of intellectual property debates ultimately devolve to who gets paid how much and when, the mechanism for assuring fair compensation—a limited monopoly right—has profound consequences for the circulation and availability of cultural artifacts.

Further, I've come to sense that the actions of the participants in these debates speak more generally to the nature and character of the U.S. political process. These debates offer a window into how policy is set in the U.S., and the understanding drawn from these debates is helpful when one wishes to understand the often-convoluted machinations of the U.S. Congress as it works to make law, or when one endeavors to extract some measure of reason from the latest Federal verdict in a copyright case. Given the U.S.'s current position as an international superpower, the machinations of Congressional leadership radiate well beyond this country's borders. My hope is that by offering a clear account of the politics of persuasion in a debate I'm especially equipped to interpret, I will also offer readers a sharpened sense of the current state of political persuasion in our media-saturated era.

In part, the curious nature of the peer-to-peer debates reflects the unusual politics of intellectual property within the U.S. This was driven home for me during my travels as a teacher. In the summer of 2000, I journeyed to Ukraine for three weeks as part of an international teaching team. During the trip I had a brief opportunity to live in a culture largely untouched by Western intellectual property laws, and this affected many elements of my stay.

Our Ukrainian hosts were extremely generous with the limited computer resources they had, which felt slow and cumbersome to a spoiled U.S. academic used to DSL and T1 lines plugged into his home and office computers. Most of the computers I used in Ukraine were running on pirated copies of Microsoft's Windows operating system, and the pirated copies were sometimes incomplete. At our first stop, in Dniepropetrovsk, I reoriented myself to the Web and e-mail at dial-up speeds. The Internet had become my medium of choice for communicating with friends and family, as the costs and logistical hurdles involved in making international telephone calls were discouraging, to say the least. (I recall paying what I perceived to be a fair sum for what I thought was a 200 minute phone card, only to dial home and watch the 200 *seconds* I had purchased tick down on the phone's LED display.) So, over the course of my stay, I ultimately relied on e-mail to keep in contact with my wife, friends, and family. Because the bootleg Windows operating system on the local computers was well-removed from any opportunities for legal technical support, the computers were maintained by immensely talented programmers (most of whom appeared to be in their early twenties) who developed software-based bridges whenever they were needed to prop up the operating system. Thus the Windows OS—an emphatically proprietary product in the U.S.—was functioning on the model of open source software, with hackers revising, patching, and improving the software to meet the specific needs of Ukrainian users.

At our second stop, in Uzhgorod, my colleagues and I depended on a small computer lab stocked with underpowered Windows-based computers all sharing a single telephone connection. While I had settled into managing with diminished processing speed in Dniepropetrovsk, the Uzhgorod lab connections were much slower, and over time I discovered why. In addition to e-mail exchanges and Web surfing, the student technicians managing the lab had queued an enormous number of MP3 files for downloading to the lab's fastest machine. While we were struggling to compose and send out our daily updates to our loved ones, Marilyn Manson's latest eruptions were streaming in.

At the end of the Ukraine trip I had the opportunity to briefly visit Kiev's city center. In one subway station, I saw a salesman with a table full of jewel-cased discs. Many of the discs contained obviously counterfeit versions of popular software programs, but the remainder were music discs, albeit unlike any I had ever seen in the States. Many of the music discs were also obviously counterfeit, featuring the same obvious flaws seen in pirated CDs sold in major U.S. cities: blurry reproductions of cover and disc art, absence of a complete booklet, and cheap paper stock. But there was also a "brand" (of sorts) of compact disc, with songs recorded in MP3 format, which featured *all* of the records (to that date) released by particular performers. I purchased three of these discs, released by a company calling itself "Domoshnyaya Kollektsia" (roughly "Home Collection" and hereinafter, simply DK), paying roughly $10, U.S. for each disc. The disc for alternative rock band R.E.M. comprehensively collected *all* of its official releases, from a 1982 debut E.P. to the 1998 album, "Up." The disc for producer and ex-Roxy Music member Brian Eno similarly encompassed fifteen albums from 1973 to 1998. But the most impressive disc was the Iggy Pop collection, which incorporated the three official album releases of Pop's work as a member of the Stooges, sixteen of Pop's subsequent albums, a tribute album to Pop, and, for good measure, a song

Figure 1. The Ukrainian Iggy Pop MP3 Collection.

Pop had contributed to the soundtrack of the obscure movie "Arizona Dream." Several of the albums reproduced on this disc are so rare that they are nearly impossible to find in the United States.

The DK discs clearly represent the kind of piracy that major record labels dread. From their perspective, the Iggy Pop disc represents over $250 worth of retail purchases (at $15 per CD) compressed onto a single disc. These collections are by no means perfect substitutes for traditional compact discs. While the disc includes JPEG images of each of the CD booklet covers, all of the additional frills sometimes found in a CD package are missing. There are no lyrics, no songlists (as would typically be found on the "J-card" that typically functions as a CD's back cover), and the music files themselves are mid-quality MP3 files—essentially heavily compressed distillations of the original recordings.

Then again . . . close enough for rock and roll.

What the DK discs lack in visual content and elegance, they more than make up for in musical comprehensiveness and portability. While audiophiles can distinguish between compressed MP3 files and the richer source versions found on retail CDs, more typical music fans have embraced MP3 files without recognizing a significant drop-off in their enjoyment. The distinctions between CDs and MP3s, which might be apparent in an optimum listening environment quickly, evaporate when music is experienced via earbud headphones, or through computer speakers, or pumping out of a boombox. For a significant percentage of music consumers, the DK discs would be perceived as better and more useful than the legitimate releases.

It is difficult to imagine discs like these ever circulating legally in the United States. The record industry has largely succeeded in habituating consumers to the purchase of 30 to 75 minutes of music on a single disc for $15 to $20. At present, there is no real incentive for the industry to shift from this distribution model other than the clear threat posed by rampant downloading of music via the Internet. Sale of single disc MP3 collections would require a radical shift in the music industry's business models, and so far the record companies would rather fight than switch.

My trip to Ukraine offered me repeated opportunities to experience a culture that had, for a range of reasons including brute economic necessity, opted out of the Western copyright system. The practical consequences of Ukraine's failure to adhere to international copyright laws were, from a consumer perspective, largely positive. The Windows operating system, locked down by copyright in the United States, was subject to relentless hacking and tinkering in Ukraine, and the by-product was a more adaptable and flexible version of the OS. In the case of popular music, from a consumer standpoint, Ukraine is superficially preferable to the U.S. Though the MP3 CDs I purchased did not feature stellar sound quality, the discs *were* expansive, comprehensive and inexpensive, and, as such, a welcome alternative to traditional compact discs. Of course, Ukraine depends on the Western copyright regime to produce the discs that served as the bases for these pirated editions. And the content industries have argued that without fair compensation, artists will simply stop producing. The $10 MP3 CD collection is detached from the revenue stream that currently sustains record companies, retailers, and (at least in theory) recording artists. It could not become a global norm without a radical restructuring of the way content industries distribute their products and the ways these products are protected. Because the content industries generate enormous income, even with the current levels of piracy, bootlegging, and appropriation, there is limited incentive for companies to begin this restructuring process. Recent history suggests that record companies believe they are successfully shifting the terms of the peer-to-peer debates in their own favor and that they are gaining traction in their efforts to stem the tide of unauthorized peer-to-peer downloads.

The record companies may well be wrong.

In May of 2003, Kazaa Media Desktop claimed the title of "most downloaded software in the history of the Internet." By the end of that month, individuals had downloaded over 230 million copies of the file-transfer software. They did so despite persistent reports that the software included "sneakware" and "spyware'—surreptitiously installed applications that would appropriate computer processing power and monitor computer usage, sending the by-products of both back to Kazaa's parent company. Indeed, at that time the description of Kazaa Media Desktop at Download.com, one of the major sources for the software, featured the following warning:

> Editor's note: This download includes additional applications bundled with the software's installer file. Third-party applications bundled with this download may *record your surfing habits, deliver advertising, col-*

Introduction: The Cat Is Out of the Bag

> *lect private information, or modify your system settings.*
> Pay close attention to the end user license agreement and installation options. For more information, read Download.com's guide to adware.

Further, these 230 million downloads occurred despite the general understanding that Kazaa's software was designed to enable a potentially illegal activity: downloading copyrighted music and media files.

In most cases, downloads pursued by Kazaa's users were of popular music in the MP3 format. Though this format was initially developed as part of a project for compressing motion pictures (the full name of the format is "Motion Picture Experts Group Audio Layer III") the format proved exceptionally useful for the transmission of audio files. When the format was developed in 1995, few computers had the high-bandwidth connections needed to transmit full motion video files, which measured in the hundreds of megabytes no matter how dramatic the compression. But audio files, when compressed via the MP3 format, typically measured between three and six megabytes of data. Files of this size could be transferred over dial-up connections in under ten minutes, and, on high-speed connections, a single song would typically download in well under a minute.

The American public has since demonstrated a voracious appetite for MP3 and MP3-type music files and has persisted in using peer-to-peer networks to download music despite the implicit threats to privacy posed by Kazaa and the possible illegality of their actions (as implied by the injunction that closed Napster as a "free" peer-to-peer network). This book addresses the questions raised by the American public's continuing and expanding use of peer-to-peer technologies in spite of ongoing campaigns to characterize peer-to-peer downloads as criminal behavior. While the majority of the public now seems to have been persuaded that their actions might well be illegal, they aren't buying the larger argument—that they must cease and desist downloading. Nor, apparently, are they buying as many compact discs as they once did, though this may or may not be attributable to peer-to-peer downloading.

For the Internet to reach its full potential, content must be affordable, available, and readily accessible. At present, copyright law is functioning as an obstacle to use and circulation of material throughout the Internet, despite its foundational imperative—as expressed in the U.S. Constitution—to "promote the progress of science and useful arts." In her 2001 book *Digital Copyright,* legal scholar Jessica Litman argues that existing law has become too complex for this purpose:

> If ordinary people are to see copyrights as equivalents to tangible property and accord copyright rules the respect they give to other property rules, then we would need, at a minimum, to teach them the rules that govern intellectual property when we teach them the rules that govern other personal property, which is to say in elementary school. The problem, though, is that our current copyright statute could not be taught in elementary school, because elementary school students couldn't understand it. Indeed, their teachers couldn't understand it. Copyright lawyers don't understand it. (*Digital* 58)

Litman ends her book by concluding: "people don't obey laws that they don't believe in" (195). And indeed, to the extent that average American citizens engage with intellectual property laws, they understand them to be maddeningly complex, unfair, or insignificant, or some combination of all three.

This concern becomes particularly pronounced when one acknowledges that the principal users of peer-to-peer technologies for music and motion picture downloads are college students. Major research universities were among the first institutions to make the significant investments in networking technologies needed to make peer-to-peer transfers viable. At present, universities are competing with one another to offer ever-faster broadband and wireless Internet access throughout their campuses. A generation of students is growing accustomed to the expectation that high-speed Internet access will be available to them whenever they open their laptops. Many (if not most) of these students regard copyright law with a learned sense of contempt.

In the modern research university we see widespread high-speed Internet access colliding with the general academic culture of relatively free circulation of information. While students and their families pay increasingly exorbitant tuition, once these bills are paid, students have effectively free access to an astonishing array of cultural artifacts. A good research library, when paired with digital access to proprietary databases like LEXIS-NEXIS (as is common on most campuses), means students can pursue their research questions by locating full text articles from most of the magazines on a typical newsstand, almost all of the world's major newspapers, and the ever-increasing number of academic journals serving disciplines from aerobiology to zootomy. The value and volume of material circulating "freely" on college campuses has soared exponentially with the advent of the Internet. And this largely unlimited access to information is dependent upon U.S. copyright law's acknowledgment that "progress" depends on a balance between private monopolies and public access. Because they are so dependent upon research, academic institutions, for better and for worse, are the spaces in which the limits of intellectual property law are recalibrated, reevaluated, and, sometimes, revised. But academics have not always fully recognized their special obligation to shape debates over intellectual property policies.

Since the mid-1970s, U.S. academics have come to rely on what is known as the "fair use exception" to copyright law. The exception codified a widely recognized principle that educational institutions and libraries ought to be granted some leeway in their uses of copyrighted materials. The 1976 revision of the U.S. Copyright Act specifies "criticism, comment, news reporting, teaching (including multiple copies for classroom use), scholarship,[and] research" as special activities wherein users may be entitled to make substantial use of copyrighted materials without making payment or securing permission (17 U.S. Code, sec. 107). The revision outlines a four-point test to be applied by courts on a case-by-case basis to determine whether a given use is a "fair use or infringement." Courts are directed to consider:

1. the purpose and character of the use, including whether such use is of a commercial nature or is for nonprofit educational purposes;
2. the nature of the copyrighted work;
3. the amount and substantiality of the portion used in relation to the copyrighted work as a whole; and
4. the effect of the use upon the potential market for or value of the copyrighted work.

Under the 1976 fair use doctrine, a classroom instructor at a public university distributing multiple copies of an excerpt from a copyrighted article drawn from a disciplinary journal (thereby potentially stimulating interest in the work and thus enhancing its value) would almost certainly have been judged to have made a fair use of the copyrighted material. But if that same instructor were to compile a coursepack of whole articles for a third party to sell to students, courts might well find—as a federal district court found in the 1991 case *Basic Books v. Kinko's*—that such a compilation is too commercial, that it incorporates too much (i.e., all) of the copyrighted works, and that it will likely have a negative effect on the values of the copyrighted works, and, thus, is an infringing use of those articles.

As the *Basic Books* decision implies, the three decades since the codification of fair use have been marked by increasingly circumscribed opportunities for public access to and use of copyrighted materials and by a radical shift in the general perception of what might constitute reasonable and legal use of protected works. One among many examples will serve to illustrate this shift. Universities have, for decades, been experimenting with long-distance delivery of their instruction to affiliated campuses and students. Prior to 2002, instructors in distance education classrooms might reasonably have presumed that the rules established for face-to-face classrooms would be maintained for distance delivery. If, for example, an instructor determined that the class would be best served by screening a film, the instructor would almost certainly have concluded that the "safe harbor" offered by fair use, especially the allowance of "multiple copies for classroom use" would eliminate the likelihood of a copyright conflict. The 2002 passage of the TEACH Act, however, radically complicates the decision-making process for all instructors involved in distance education. The above-cited four-point fair use test has been widely criticized for its complexity and for its inability to produce definitive determinations as to whether a given use is fair until a case is litigated, but the 1976 Act's fair use "test" is a model of clarity when measured against the TEACH Act's network of interlocking standards and guidelines. The legalese of the act itself is alarmingly incomprehensible. Because the Act itself is so abstruse, universities are endeavoring to provide guidance to those teachers who persist in wishing to make use of copyrighted materials in their classrooms. For example, the University of Texas's "Crash Course in Copyright" features a Web-based guide to the TEACH Act and offers this helpful gloss on the new standards instructors should employ to determine whether a given use of copyrighted material is permitted by the TEACH Act:

Introduction: The Cat Is Out of the Bag 17

1. The performance or display must be:
    a. A regular part of systematic mediated instructional activity;
    b. Made by, at the direction of, or under the supervision of the instructor;
    c. Directly related and of material assistance to the teaching content; and
    d. For and technologically limited to students enrolled in the class.
2. The institution must:
    a. Have policies and provide information about, and give notice that the materials used may be protected by, copyright;
    b. Apply technological measures that reasonably prevent recipients from retaining the works beyond the class session and further distributing them; and
    c. Not interfere with technological measures taken by copyright owners that prevent retention and distribution. (Harper)

Any distance education instructor without the patience of Job would quickly conclude that the requirements of the TEACH Act far outweigh the benefits of making use of copyrighted materials. Indeed, the Act seems designed to present a series of obstacles to use, and also to tacitly encourage instructors to forego making use of copyrighted materials altogether. The above-cited steps 2.a. and 2.b., both fair summaries of the Act's requirements, place instructors in the uncomfortable position of policing their institutions' compliance with the TEACH Act. If an instructor determines that her academic institution has not yet established clear policies with respect to copyright and not yet provided ample notice of copyright protections to students, the TEACH Act discourages her from making use of copyrighted material in the classroom and implicitly encourages her to begin instigating institutional changes.

A dutiful instructor who keeps abreast of intellectual property policies and teaches in distance education classrooms ends up engaging students in conversations like this:

> *Instructor*: At this point, I had hoped to show the film *Desk Set*, which ably speaks to the questions of gender and tech-

nology that we've been addressing in this class, but due to the provisions of the TEACH Act, I'm afraid I will not be showing it in class, though I encourage you to watch it on your own time, if you can get your hands on a copy . . .

Student: Is it available online?

Instructor: Not legally. There is a copy at our library, but there are no copies at the distance sites.

Student: So why can't you show it in class?

Instructor: I'm not sure I can meet the TEACH Act's requirement that I somehow prevent additional copies being derived from the "broadcast" of the film across our campuses.

Student: (peering up from an open laptop) I just looked that movie up on Amazon. It's only eight bucks used. What if I buy it and rip DVD copies for everyone who can't get it from their library? Then you can send them the copies and we can discuss the film later this semester . . .

Instructor: That's a very generous offer, but the TEACH Act really is directed at ensuring that copies of copyrighted materials don't get into circulation, so I probably shouldn't forward them . . .

Student: OK, how about this? You call in sick on Thursday. I'll go up to the podium, hook up my laptop and screen the library's copy of the movie. Then you come back Tuesday and we'll discuss the movie.

Instructor: As pleased as I am with your apparent interest in this fifty-year-old film, the point of the law is to prevent the kinds of distributions you're talking about, even though we often screen films in face-to-face classrooms. Apparently, Congress was really concerned about schools facilitating the widespread copying and circulation of copyrighted materials.

Student: But this isn't like when we watch *Spider-Man* in a friend's dorm room. It's not just entertainment. You want us to discuss and criticize what's in the film, right? That's part of the "educational process," right?

Instructor: That's the idea, yes.

> *Student*: And we can't do that because we're in a distance classroom? But you could screen the film in a regular class?
> *Instructor*: That's how I interpret the law.
> *Student*: That's bullshit!

This is a lightly fictionalized distillation of a number of conversations I have had with students over the past few years. While profanity is neither common nor encouraged in my classrooms, discussions of copyright inevitably seem to end up with a student arriving at this precise expletive to describe the strictures of copyright law. And, we should note, the TEACH Act is functionally amending laws that date back to the U.S.'s first copyright law, entitled "An Act for the Encouragement of Learning, by securing the Copies of Maps, Charts and Books to the Authors and Proprietors of such Copies during the Times therein mentioned." The text of the TEACH Act is all the evidence one would ever need that U.S. Copyright law is now well removed from any meaningful "encouragement of learning."

Peer-to-peer technologies, when paired with the T1-line access to the Internet offered by most universities and colleges, offer a sharp counterpoint to increasingly constrained classroom environments. Students (albeit at their own peril) are surfing a vast media library whose riches rival those envisioned by Jorge Luis Borges in his universally comprehensive (and necessarily fictional) "Library of Babel." They live in dormitories where access to cultural artifacts is functionally unlimited, so long as one turns a blind eye toward copyright law. But they work in classrooms where instructors are constrained from making the kinds of choices they once made without apprehension because it is legally risky for *institutions* to turn a willfully blind eye toward copyright law.

If academics fail to make persuasive cases for the ethical and reasonable uses of copyrighted materials in their classrooms, they are contributing to a culture in which copyright law remains both inexplicable and widely disregarded by the general public. Academia's failure to mount a campaign strong enough to block the plainly unworkable TEACH Act (along with the attendant failures to prevent a twenty-year extension to the term of copyright and the unduly harsh penalties of the Digital Millennium Copyright Act) have practical consequences for the digitally engaged students of the twenty-first century. Because even the most reasonable and ethical uses of copyrighted materials trigger copyright concerns, these students are concluding, like Dickens's Mr. Bumble, that "the law is a ass—a idiot." And, incidentally, Dickens's Bumble is well-known and often quoted in the U.S. largely because books like *Oliver Twist* were sold in cheap pirated editions throughout the U.S. in the mid-to-late nineteenth Century.

The U.S.'s adherence to general principles of international copyright has been fitful, and this nation's heavy emphasis on the public benefit (as opposed to rewarding effort by authors and inventors) is anomalous in an international context. For many years, the U.S.'s approach to copyright has been largely successful, fueling considerable successes in publishing, film, and music. But at present, I stand with many notable scholars in the fields of rhetoric, composition, literature, cultural studies, and legal studies (among them Dan Burk, Rebecca Moore Howard, Peter Jaszi, Karen Burke LeFevre, Lawrence Lessig, Jessica Litman, Andrea Lunsford, James E. Porter, Jacqueline Jones Royster, Siva Vaidhyanathan, and Martha Woodmansee) who have argued that in the past few decades, the U.S. has lost the balance that fueled these successes and that current law no longer serves the Constitutional call for promotion of science and useful arts as effectively as it should.

My sense is that the effort to develop informed policies with respect to access to and use of information via the Internet will benefit greatly by increased attention to the language used to shape these policies. With this in mind, each of the five core chapters of this book addresses a key term or metaphoric frame at or near the center of the peer-to-peer debates.

Methodologically, I describe this book as a work of rhetorical historicism. My approach is rooted in the subset of rhetorical criticism Edwin Black referred to as historical criticism, focused on the tasks of "authentication of texts and their interpretation in the light of biographical, social, and ideological evidence" (37). I undertake these tasks guided by Michel Foucault's admonitions, embedded in his description of his archaeological method, to evaluate rhetorical performances by paying particular attention to who is speaking, to the institutional sites authorizing discourse, and to the situation of the subject within social networks (51–53). My efforts to analyze and critique particular rhetorical actions and their relationships within their broader cultural contexts do not correspond precisely to Foucault's archaeological and genealogical methods, but they do resonate with two critical practices that are rooted in Foucault's methodology: Steven Mailloux's rhetorical hermeneutics and Stephen Greenblatt's new historicism. Mailloux describes rhetorical hermeneutics as a practice of "tak[ing] an historical act of interpretation [. . .] and do[ing] a rhetorical analysis of the cultural conversations in which that act participated" ("Revisited" 238–39) or, more epigrammatically, "us[ing] rhetoric to practice theory by doing history" ("Revisited" 233). Rhetorical hermeneutics encourages critics to read particular rhetorical actions in terms of their participation in broader cultural networks, thereby offering a greater balance between text and context than competing critical methods. Similarly, Greenblatt's new historicism interprets particular literary texts in terms of contemporaneous texts and circumstances, seeking to understand particular texts not as transcending their cultural conversations, but as embedded within and responding to them. Both rhetorical hermeneutics and new historicism encourage particular attention to the operations of cultural power as effected through language. My *rhetorical* historicism shares an attention to the operations of power in cultural contexts, but with a particular focus on key terms and how their meanings are transformed by particular rhetorical agents over time, rather than on texts and their relationships to one another.

The peer-to-peer debates are rich with contested terms. This book focuses on five terms that have served as focal points for the competing parties in these debates. When these terms are read with attention to their position in broader cultural networks, it becomes clear that the rhetoric of the peer-to-peer debates fails to meet the ethical and logical standards that have long been acknowledged by those who study persuasion. Over the course of this book's central chapters, I argue that the past decade's presentations of peer-to-peer file transfers as "hacking," "theft," "piracy," "sharing," and "war," consistently distort both the technologies and the social behaviors they purport to describe.

By aggressively interrogating the language and the arguments deployed by participants in the peer-to-peer debates, I seek to elevate the discourse at the heart of this important conversation. Digital media offer opportunities to efficiently archive and access the bulk of artistic and intellectual work created since the dawn of humanity. *This is not an overstatement.* The potential intellectual and social utility of these now-hypothetical archives is staggering. Our challenge is to engage in a principled argument about how best to achieve this goal. To date, as this book will document, the rhetoric of the peer-to-peer debates suggests that we have yet to meet this challenge.

2 Hackers, Crackers, and the Criminalization of Peer-to-Peer Technologies

Of all the shifting, fluid terms used to describe the Internet and its associated cultures, no term is more contested than "hacker." The resonances embedded within this term not only proved critical to the outcome of the Napster case, they also continue to shape the U.S.'s dialogue on whether peer-to-peer technologies should remain legal. Peer-to-peer technologies have, effectively, been tarred by their lingering association with the questionable practices of hackers, or, more properly, the subset of hackers known in some circles as "crackers."

In this chapter, I adapt Stephen Mailloux's rhetorical hermeneutics to illuminate the shifting meanings ascribed to the word, "hacker" and the social forces responsible for those shifts. As Mailloux explains, rhetorical hermeneutics "views shared interpretive strategies not as the creative origin of texts but rather as historical sets of topics, arguments, tropes, ideologies, and so forth which determine how texts are established as meaningful through rhetorical exchange" (*Power* 15). The strategy at the heart of the approach Mailloux outlines is ably summarized by Michael Leff as "thick descriptions of interpretative practices that are mindful of the shifting political positions of those who engage in them" (197). Accordingly, this chapter will offer a thick description of the historical circumstances surrounding the early usage and subsequent repurposings of the term "hacker."

Tracing the shifts in the meaning of "hacker" provides a lens with which we can understand the larger cultural shifts associated with the Internet and with peer-to-peer technologies in particular. To do so, we must work our way back to an understanding of what *hacker* meant to those who coined and used the term before it entered the general public's vocabulary. Once this baseline is established, it will be possible to interrogate *why* the meaning of the term has shifted so dramatically, and more importantly, *who* might be responsible for this shift. This chapter argues, in part, that shifts in the meanings of key terms relating to computers and the Internet do not simply evolve. Rather, they are contested sites where interested parties struggle to frame the activities at the heart of the term according to their preferences and perceived needs.

In the introduction to his 2002 book *Hacker Culture,* Douglas Thomas writes that "the very definition of the term 'hacker' is widely and fiercely disputed by both critics of and participants in the computer underground" (ix). In a similar vein, in the preface to his 2001 book, *The Hacker Ethic,* Pekka Himanen offers a compressed account of the key shifts in the use of the term:

> [A] group of MIT's passionate programmers started calling themselves hackers in the early sixties. (Later, in the mid-eighties, the media started applying the term to computer criminals. In order to avoid the confusion with virus writers and intruders into information systems, hackers began calling these destructive computer users *crackers*. (vii-viii)

But Himanen's account is problematic, in that even the first generation hackers have a demonstrable history of "intruding into information systems." In fact, one of the earliest references to "hackers" is found in a November, 1963, edition of *The Tech,* MIT's campus newspaper. The article reports:

> The hackers have accomplished such things as tying up all the tie-lines between Harvard and MIT, or making long-distance calls by charging them to a local radar installation. One method involved connecting the PDP-1 computer to the phone system to search the lines until a dial tone, indicating an outside line, was found. (Lichstein)

While these activities border on the kind of collegiate hijinks sometimes dismissed as youthful indiscretions, there was also a clear sense that these early hackers were violating the law. A quotation ascribed to MIT Professor Carlton Tucker reflects the academy's apparent ambivalence toward these activities:

> Tucker said "If any of these people are caught (by the telephone company) they are liable to be put in jail. I try to warn them and protect them." While Tucker felt "we don't have too much trouble with the boys; we appreciate their curiosity," he also said that repeated involvement, for instance, caused the expulsion from the Institute of one member of the Class of '63 one week before his graduation. (Lichstein)

Tucker's language clearly implies that he viewed the penalties likely to be exacted by the telephone company and/or the law as excessive. Further, he suggests that the university would reserve its most severe punishment—expulsion—for those "boys" who *repeatedly* engaged in the activities described, presumably in the interest of encouraging the curiosity these hackers apparently exemplified.

Ultimately the distinction Himanen attempts to draw between the first generation of hackers and later so-called crackers hinges on a judgment with respect to the participants' overall intent. First generation hackers' intrusions are understood as *generally* benign and exploratory in nature, while the activities of those labeled "crackers" are understood as, by definition, destructive. Small wonder, then, that efforts to recover an "originary" meaning for the term "hacker" have proven demonstrably unsuccessful. For the lay public, the meaning of the term is clear, and clearly negative. A hacker is an individual who deploys advanced knowledge of computers and the Internet in order to invade others' machines. While the purpose of the hacker's invasion might range from exploration to identity theft, the signature elements in the generally understood uses of the term hacker are *criminal trespass.* The hacker violates someone else's (virtual) property rights without permission.

While it is already difficult to recall in full the culture and language of the first wave of hackers, there are a number of texts that function effectively as "time capsules," offering snapshots of early hackers and their activities. Among the most important of these is a 1984 book by Steven Levy with the telling title, *Hackers: Heroes of the Computer Revolution.* Levy's choice of "heroes" is underscored by the paperback edition's front cover blurb, which reads, "What Tom Wolfe did for the original astronauts, Steven Levy has done for hackers." Implicit in this comparison is the suggestion that hackers, like astronauts, are *explor-*

ers. Levy himself makes this connection in his preface, referring to hackers as "digital explorers" and writing:

> Though some in the field used the term "hacker" as a form of derision, implying that hackers were either nerdy social outcasts or "unprofessional" programmers who wrote dirty, "nonstandard" computer code, I found them quite different. Beneath their often unimposing exteriors, they were adventurers, visionaries, risk takers, artists [. . .] and the ones who most clearly saw why the computer was a revolutionary tool. Among themselves, they knew how far one could go by immersion into the deep concentration of the hacking mind-set: one could go infinitely far. (7)

Levy's rhetorical flourishes indicate the degree to which he, and many of his contemporaries (including the hackers themselves), positioned the first generation of hackers as successors to the exploratory spirit embodied in the NASA astronauts. NASA's last manned mission to the moon was in December of 1972. The space shuttle program, a comparatively modest endeavor, did not launch its first manned mission until 1981, and five years later, the explosion of the Columbia spacecraft would radically alter a generation's perceptions of the possibilities and risks of exploring space. Thus, when the first generation of hackers reached the public's consciousness in the mid-1970s—the U.S.'s exploration of what had once been described as "the final frontier" had waned dramatically. NASA was no longer minting a steady supply of astronaut heroes, nor was it able to offer steady reassurance of the U.S.'s technological superiority. The plaque on one of the legs of the Eagle moon landing module reads: "Here men from the planet Earth first set foot upon the moon. July 1969 A.D. We came in peace for all mankind," bespeaking an expansive ambition that features—embedded within its language—a wish for a more unified global culture.

Though the astronauts *did* plant the U.S. flag on the moon's surface (arguably the most dramatic property claim in human history) the plaque's language avoids referencing the event as a specifically *American* triumph—a choice that is striking given the degree to which the "space race" was a tethered to the Cold War politics of the time. When, three years later, NASA terminated the Apollo program, canceling three scheduled missions (Apollos 18–20) the U.S. was, for a time, left with no real outlet for the exploratory impulse that, since at least Lewis and Clark, has been celebrated as fundamental to the nation's ethos.

Levy's account of the first generation of hackers not only expressly positions hackers as the latest in a long line of American explorers, it also suggests stridently that their motivations, like those of the astronauts, were ultimately to offer something of value "for all mankind." This is especially apparent in Levy's codification of the "Hacker Ethic," a summation of the shared principles adhered to by the majority of the first generation of hackers. According to Levy, the generally recognized principles of the Hacker Ethic were:

- Access to computers—and anything which might teach you something about the way the world works—should be unlimited and total.
- Always yield to the Hands-on Imperative!
- All information should be free.
- Mistrust authority—promote decentralization.
- Hackers should be judged by their hacking, not bogus criteria such as degrees, age, race or position.
- You can create art and beauty on a computer.
- Computers can change your life for the better. (39–45)

In Levy's articulation of the Hacker Ethic it is possible to trace the convergence of the U.S.'s historic valorization of exploration, exemplified at the time by the space program, with the idealistic social visions that grew out of the youth culture of the 1960s. While at first blush, the quasi-militaristic personae of the astronauts would appear to be wholly at odds with the politics of hippie/yippie cultures, both NASA and hippie leaders foregrounded their commitments to exploration in their personal and public presentations. While there is (almost) a world of difference between the Eagle lunar lander and the Merry Pranksters' psychedelic tour bus, both share a commitment to traveling as far as possible, whether it be in outer space or "inner space."

Histories of the Internet have long acknowledged the degree to which the architects of the Internet understood their work as an extension of the countercultural movements of the 1960s. In his expansive account of the Internet's development, *Nerds 2.01,* Stephen Segaller argues that hippie culture thoroughly permeated the Internet throughout its first decade.

Indeed, the language of Levy's Hacker Ethic has rhetorical roots that extend back at least as far as the 1962 Port Huron Statement, in which the college-age members of Students for a Democratic Society set the agenda for the tumultuous decade to follow, writing:

> Men have unrealized potential for self-cultivation, self-direction, self-understanding, and creativity. It is this potential that we regard as crucial and to which we appeal, not to the human potentiality for violence, unreason, and submission to authority. The goal of man and society should be human independence. (Hayden, et al.)

Like the members of SDS and the youth movements that arose alongside it, members of the first generation of hackers often had a vexed relationship with the law. The collective commitment to "mistrust[ing] authority" carried with it an at times casual disregard for the legal principles that function as an expression of cultural authority. Further, the high cultural value associated with exploration prompted hacker forays into electronic spaces where they were at best unwelcome and at worst criminal.

In 1994, Levy composed an afterword for a new edition of *Hackers* in which he acknowledges that even the first generation of hackers— the hackers he celebrates as "true hackers"—were not consistently respectful of the laws governing their activities. Levy writes:

> True, some of the most righteous hackers in history have been known to sneer at details such as property rights or the legal code in order to pursue the Hands-On Imperative. And pranks have always been part of hacking. But the inference that such high jinks [sic] were the essence of hacking was not just wrong, it was offensive to true hackers, whose work had changed the world, and whose methods could change the way one viewed the world. (433)

Levy's argument is that the transgressions of the first generation of hackers should be understood (and implicitly, should be dismissed) because these actions were peripheral to the larger goals of "changing the world." Again, the judgment hinges on a determination with respect to the hackers' intent, but in place of Professor Tucker's "boys will be boys" defense, we have Levy's rather grandiose suggestion that the hackers' visitation of others' computers was participating in an expansive process of positive global transformation.

One hacker who arguably deserves Levy's hyperbole is Richard Stallman, whose has worked for two decades as the leader and inspiration for the "Free Software" movement and the chief developer of "GNU," a resolutely free alternative to the proprietary UNIX operating system. Like Levy, Stallman cites "playfulness, cleverness, and exploration" as the signature elements of true hacking (15). Stallman's own account of his efforts bespeaks an idealism rooted in the 1960s counterculture, and an overarching commitment to building community via electronic spaces. Stallman traces his interest in developing GNU to the dissolution of the rich community of first and second generation hackers that surrounded him as he pursued his college education in the early 1970s. After mourning this loss, Stallman determined to take action: "I looked for a way that a programmer could do something for the good. I asked myself, was there a program or programs that I could write, so as to make a community possible once again?" (17) Stallman's "general public license," which assures that the by-products of the GNU Project will circulate under parallel (i.e., free) license agreements, has served as a model for a generation of academics and programmers, including the prominent legal scholar Lawrence Lessig. Lessig's Creative Commons foundation adapts the principles of Stallman's software licenses and applies them to the broad range of "properties" subject to copyright protection, offering creators multiple opportunities to opt out of copyright's more problematic "protections." Stallman's expansive vision remains obscure if measured in terms of market share, but highly significant if evaluated in terms of "mind share" among academics and others committed to transforming intellectual property policies in favor of public access.

Relative to Stallman's efforts, the achievements of hippie-inflected hacking often appear rather modest. While self-identified hackers were responsible for developing most of the elements of the Internet, Segaller's history observes that one of the most popular uses of the early Internet network known as the WELL was the facilitation of trades of cassette-tape recordings of the Grateful Dead. Segaller writes:

> By 1984, as the Macintosh was launched, the hippie origins of networking were once again beginning to show themselves. Part of the impetus came from an electronic version of the Whole Earth Catalog (whose Epilog had come and gone a decade earlier). Inevitably, it was Stewart Brand who originated and branded what he called the "Whole Earth 'Lectronic Link," or WELL. Now more users were able to tune in and turn on to the highs of networking, attracted by the chance to connect with like-minded people—even "Dead" people. One should not underestimate the importance in the history of the Internet of the Grateful Dead. (269)

The Grateful Dead, of course, holds special significance in the prehistory of the peer-to-peer debate. The Dead's pioneering toleration of fans taping its concerts and subsequently trading the tapes is routinely pointed to as a potentially viable model for the kinds of contemporary exchanges of digital media made possible by peer-to-peer technologies. The band forbade the unauthorized *sale* of concert tapes, but encouraged fans to trade with one another, and thereby became one of the most successful touring bands ever. And the latter portion of the band's career was unquestionably enhanced by the emergence of a technologically engaged fan base that would leverage the Internet in support of their Dead-focused activities. While the streamlining of cassette distribution is of limited cultural value, it is fortuitous that the modes and models established by this community radiated out throughout the WELL and ultimately, the Internet itself.

The WELL was instrumental in demonstrating the possibility and potential of online communities. At a time when the foundational 1960s efforts to explore outer and inner spaces had surrendered to the cultural malaise of the mid-1970s, the exploration of what would come to be known as cyberspace offered exciting opportunities for a certain stripe of explorer. While not everyone would agree that the Internet offers "changed views of the world," a generation of scholarship on the Internet has increasingly acknowledged the importance and value of the kinds of communities instantiated by first generation hackers in electronic spaces like the WELL.

Whether or not one accepts these celebratory accounts of first generation hackers, the critical question raised by Levy's recapitulation of the idealistic rhetoric of the time is this: By what means were the admittedly illicit but arguably harmless activities of Levy's "true hackers" supplanted, in the public's consciousness, by the putatively criminal activities of a subsequent wave? That this shift in meaning occurred, somewhere between the 1970s and the mid-1990s, is acknowledged by nearly all who write about the history of hacking. Levy ascribes the shift to the term's increasing popularity blended with a kind of bad luck, in which self-described hackers who either misunderstood or ignored the spirit of the Hacker Ethic assumed center stage owing to the ignorance of the mainstream media:

> [F]or many true hackers [. . .] the popularization of the term was a disaster. Why? The word hacker had acquired a specific and negative connotation. The trouble began with some well-publicized arrests of teenagers who electronically ventured into forbidden digital grounds, like government computer systems. It was understandable that the journalists covering these stories would refer to the young perps as hackers—after all that's what the kids called *themselves*. But the word quickly became synonymous with "digital trespasser." (432)

But it is only the *publicity* associated with the arrests that distinguishes these "young perps" from their hacker forebears. Government computer systems have long been attractive targets for hackers. Those hackers whose ethical stance mandates exploration without disturbing the sites they "visit" typically argue that government sites typically house the most elaborate and, thus, most compelling aggregations of software and hardware. These cathedrals of code have proven irresistible to generations of hackers—but first generation hackers were the beneficiaries of lax enforcement and general ignorance about computer security. In Levy's account, the shift in the meaning of the word "hacker" is attributable to a combination of happenstance, ignorance, and error. Thus, Levy offers little to those striving for "thick descriptions that are mindful of the shifting political positions of those who engage in [interpretative practices]" (Leff, 197). Levy's account ignores the questions of agency and accountability for this shift, thereby implying that something like a "natural evolution" had transpired.

By contrast, Andrew Ross's 1990 article "Hacking Away at the Counterculture" offers a bracingly specific account of not only the shift in the meaning of the term, but also a clear identification (or, more properly *accusation*) of those responsible for the shift. Ross writes:

> [T]eenage hacking has come to be increasingly defined as potential threat to normative educational ethics and national security alike. The story of the creation of this "social menace" is central to the ongoing attempt to rewrite property law in order to contain the effect of the new information technologies that, because of their blindness to the copyrighting of intellectual property, have transformed the way in which modern power is exercised and maintained. Consequently, a deviant social class or group has been defined and categorized as "enemies of the state" in order to help rationalize a general law-and-order clampdown on free and open information exchange. (10)

The "state" Ross indicts here is primarily the U.S., then led by the first President Bush. And he highlights the degree to which the state depends on the maintenance of stable property lines. According to Ross, because hackers illustrate the permeability of property lines in virtual spaces, they threaten the state itself.

Ross argues that hackers represent the bleeding edge of a larger cultural conflict over the status of property in a post-digital circumstance:

> In its basic assembly structure, information technology is a technology of processing, copying, replication, and simulation, and therefore does not recognize the concept of private information property. What is now under threat is the rationality of a shareware culture, ushered in as the achievement of the hacker counterculture that pioneered the computer revolution in the early seventies against the grain of corporate planning. (9)

If one accepts Ross's argument, digital technologies are incapable of sustaining the complex array of property relations we are accustomed to in terrestrial spaces. Because digital technologies depend on duplication of data, they fundamentally compromise both the concept and the operation of property. Additionally, Ross claims that hacker culture is, by definition, anti-corporate. Ross's defense of the hacker as countercultural hero neatly explains why, by 1990, it would have been important for corporate interests to ensure that the term be repositioned as an indictment. And in December of that year, according to a front-page story in the *Washington Post,* a panel of "industry and academic experts" warned against the threat posed by hackers, describing them, in usage that now seems almost quaint, as "high-tech terrorists" (Suplee and Richards). While Ross would criticize such reporting as exemplifying a "moral panic" that threatened the "technology conscious youth culture" he valued, the term *hacker* would never recover its original meaning. The term's associations with trespass and criminality would, during the 1990s, become wholly entrenched. By the end of the decade, no thinking person who was not simultaneously announcing himself as committed to transgressing the boundaries established by a combination of corporate practice and convention would use "hacker" as a self-description.

And yet, that's just what Shawn Fanning, the principal inventor of Napster, did.

That Fanning and the coders he recruited for the Napster project saw themselves as hackers should be understood as a matter of historical fact. Though Fanning would ultimately attempt to distance himself, and by extension, Napster, from its roots in the hacker subculture, he depended on a network of fellow coders that he met through, w00w00, an online aggregation of talented third-generation hackers ("crackers" to their predecessors). Joseph Menn's *All the Rave: The Rise and Fall of Shawn Fanning's Napster* offers a window into the w00w00 culture:

> As Shawn learned more and more and worked himself up the IRC [Internet Relay Chat] hacker hierarchy, he got invited to join a private IRC channel called w00w00, which would play a key role in Nap-

ster's development. W00w00 was for hackers and others interested in security issues who knew what they were doing, having already cut their teeth elsewhere. It wasn't full of kids who pulled off hacking attacks by running scripts of code they had downloaded elsewhere. But it also wasn't for the established old-school hackers, who kept to themselves for fear of exposure. (17)

In writing that w00w00 was not "full of kids who pulled off hacking attacks by running scripts of code they had downloaded elsewhere," Menn is, importantly, *not* suggesting that w00w00's members did not attack others' computers. Rather, he is pointing up the degree to which the w00w00 culture valued the *composition*—rather than use—of scripts. Members were expected to produce rather than deploy code. And Fanning met this standard, according to Menn:

He wrote programs that took advantage of Unix computer network flaws and bore such unambiguous titles as "faker.c Dalnet Address spoofer," which allowed electronic correspondents to misrepresent their computers' locations. "Napscan.c portscanner," likewise, was a tool for checking computers for open lines to hack through. (20)

In these endeavors, Fanning was clearly pushing the limits of legal and ethical behavior. In his defense, it might also be said that he was learning the craft of coding.

Members of the hacker subculture have developed a generally recognized framework to classify one another according to the degree of risk they assume in their activities. Drawing on the old Hollywood cowboy iconography, the framework stretches from "white hats" (the good guys) to "black hats" (the villains). But unlike Hollywood cowboys, the hacker hierarchy allows for considerable nuance, as Menn demonstrates in his description of Fanning's friend and co-worker Jordan Ritter:

Ritter wasn't atypical in protecting Lehigh's computer system by day and taking it down by night. While there are plenty of white-hat security workers and black-hat malicious hackers, who assault large

> networks like Yahoo! for the thrill of it, the majority of people are in the middle, gray hats who create their own ethics. (22)

Menn goes on to identify Fanning as falling into this third category, though over time he clearly (and wisely) became selective about when he would acknowledge his past as a "gray hat" hacker:

> In his [. . .] congressional testimony, Shawn said nothing of his own hacking background—only that he was interested in programming and listening to music. When Napster was international news, every story missed the fact that Shawn was an aspiring hacker who was at best a gray hat. (20)

Menn's claim that "every story missed the fact that Shawn was an aspiring hacker," is, of course, overstated. An August 2001 article in the UK *Guardian* celebrates the degree to which Fanning embodies the stereotypical hacker: "He had left school without telling any of his teachers, and was reportedly working on it around the clock, in full *hacker* mode, with little sustenance and even less sleep" (Alderman, "FREE"; emphasis added). An October 2001 *San Francisco Chronicle* article captures a moment before Fanning and Napster wholly recognized the importance of distancing the company from Fanning's identification with the hacker subculture. Napster CEO Hank Barry even felt comfortable suggesting that a mythic "hacker" was the company's role model:

> "They may win in the short run and win in the long run legally against us, at which point Napster will be Achilles, living fast, dying young and leaving a beautiful corpse," Barry said. "We'd prefer to find our model in the original hacker Odysseus, who always found a clever way around his problems and led a long and wonderful life." (qtd. in Evangelista D1)

But while the *Chronicle* article suggests that Fanning and Napster remained comfortable with their connections to the hacker subculture, a *Time* magazine story, from the same week but focusing on the impact of the RIAA's lawsuit on the company, paints a very different picture:

Since the lawsuit began, Napster has become enveloped in something of a siege mentality, an us-vs.-them attitude toward the record labels and the press that has forced Fanning to retreat even farther into his shell. He has to monitor carefully what he says to whom and even what clothes he wears. "The cdc [the Cult of the Dead Cow, a hacker collective] guys sent me a shirt, and the lawyers told me I shouldn't wear it," he says. "It's just so tightly controlled." (Greenfeld, "Meet")

Andrew Ross suggests that hacking, by its very nature, is an anti-corporate enterprise, and here we see Fanning chafing against the restrictions that his increasingly corporate context mandated. Fanning was in the awkward position of attempting to maintain his hacker identity while simultaneously participating in Napster's increasing attempts to announce itself as a responsible corporate citizen. One tangible manifestation of the company's attempt to shed its implicit association with "black hat" hacking was the bleaching of the Napster cat logo.

Figure 2. Original and revised versions of the Napster logo. Copyright © 1999, 2001, Napster, Inc.

Menn's account of designer Sam Hanks's development of the Napster logo reveals the degree to which the original, "black cat" version was meant to reinforce Napster's rebellious, oppositional stance:

> Hanks emerged with a drawing of headphones on a face with catlike ears, eyes, and a nose. [. . .] T]he Napster crew loved it. Hanks thought he was done. But [Napster cofounder Sean Parker] called a week or so afterward, pointing out that the eyes and nose looked like a mustache and a goatee. "So I stuck in a little smirk," Hanks said. Not long afterward, Parker called again. "Some of the venture-capital guys think it looks like Satan," he said. Hanks asked what Napster users thought of it, and Parker said they loved it. "Well, who are you selling it to?" Hanks asked, exasperated. "The venture guys or the kids downloading the music?" Parker decided the logo would stay. Later, he thought that the cat image appropriately evoked stealth and thievery. Even more appropriately, he realized, cats are risk-takers who escape death. (60)

Thus, according to Menn, one of Napster's founders approved of the original black cat logo's associations with stealth and thievery, the signature charges directed against black hat hackers. Little wonder, then, that Napster's attempt to whitewash their logo and recast the black cat as a white hat did little to change the company's already established image.

As Napster's popularity swelled, the company increasingly foregrounded Fanning, encouraging the misperception that he had maintained a leadership role in the company. But Fanning occupied a fairly low position within Napster corporate structure, as reported in Trevor Merriden's 2001 book *Irresistible Forces*:

> While Shawn Fanning is still very much the public face of Napster, today he owns less than 10%, has no senior management position, isn't on the board, and isn't involved in the company's business decisions. Instead, he spends all of his time developing the company's software and acting as the company's public face. (Merriden 9)

Menn's *All the Rave* corroborates Merriden's account. Napster maintained Fanning as a figurehead and largely excluded him from both the operation and the ownership of the company his software had engendered. Given the value Fanning clearly brought to the Napster brand, this was a terrible deal, but Fanning can be excused for having made it. He agreed to the arrangement when he was *nineteen* years old.

Fanning developed the Napster code while a student at Northeastern University. Despite Fanning's having left the University almost immediately after this "Eureka" moment, the company often presented him in circumstances which reinforced a dormitory-based "hacker" persona. In a publicity photo that was featured on the company's website, a ballcap-wearing Fanning sits in front of his CD collection and what appears to be a handmade flag (a pirate flag?) looking like a sophomore with more than a touch of rebel attitude. This positioning was transpiring while the "suits" at Napster were busy preparing for the company's initial public offering, and there is an obvious gap between Napster's attempts to develop into "respectable" dot.com and the maintenance of Fanning's ethos as a blend of college-age music fan and hacker.

Figure 3. An image from Napster's website depicting Shawn Fanning in a dormitory-like setting. Copyright © 1999, Napster, Inc.

When *Time* magazine photographed Fanning for a cover story and, later, for its listing of him as one of the finalists for its person-of-the-year award, its positioning illustrates the degree to which Fanning had become synonymous with Napster. In the picture, he inhabits the headphone-wearing pose of the iconic Napster cat logo, and the accompanying text points out that "Napster" is both the company's name and a childhood nickname for Fanning. The line between Fanning and the company is further blurred by the title of the October 2000 article, "Meet the Napster." While likely intended as a play on the cultural tremors that arose in response to "Meet the Beatles," the title also underscores the extent to which Fanning functioned as the embodiment of a corporation well removed from his interests and control.

Given Fanning's intractable association with the by-then marginalized, if not *demonized* figure of the hacker, one wonders why the company continued to foreground him. Fanning was quickly stripped of many of the benefits that typically accrue to inventors by the leaders of the Napster corporation. But Fanning was expected to maintain his identity as the *author* of Napster, even as the company moved away from his initial vision for the software. Because Fanning's nickname was embedded within the corporation, his identity would, for better or worse, shape the popular understanding of the company.

While Napster clearly recognized the dangers presented by Fanning's continuing identification with the hacker subculture, the company also realized that the implicitly transgressive aspects of Fanning's public persona offered Napster a point of connection with its anticipated users. A hastily-produced book-length biography of Fanning summarizes the key points of connection he offered to Napster's users: "Part of Shawn Fanning's appeal was that he embodied the look and attitude of America's youth culture. He wore baggy clothes, loved swapping MP3s, and was irreverent when it came to big business telling him what to do" (Mitten 64). While Napster's corporate structure was often marred by confusion and disarray, the company proved remarkably effective in developing a consistent company ethos, grounded in the iconic figures of the Napster cat and the cat's human counterpart, Shawn Fanning.

Classical treatments of ethos cannot wholly account for the ways in which Napster established its connections with an audience. Clearly, Napster's stance toward its intended audience was not one grounded in the establishment of the Aristotelian triad of good sense (*phronesis*) virtue (*arête*) and good will (*eunoia*), as the company's presentation is grounded, in large part, on a violation of the established order. Rather, Napster's appeals to its audience were grounded in an "outlaw" ethos, which obliged the company to foreground its opposition to the music industry's "business as usual." Napster had t-shirt-wearing fans not because the company was sensible or virtuous, but because it announced itself as an avenue for rebellion, for blows against the empire. Indeed, Napster was participating in the same sort of anti-authoritarian stance that has become conventional within the rock and hip-hop genres. As fans proclaimed, "Napster rocks," this obliged Napster to maintain an orientation toward its fans and join in their rage against the perceived corporate machine even as it strove to stabilize its own corporate machinery.

Michael Coyle and John Dolan's 1999 article "Modeling Authenticity, Authenticating Commercial Models" illustrates the kind of polarities that rock musicians face when turning toward the marketplace:

> New sounds are invariably proclaimed as liberations from the devitalizing control of industry, even as such proclamation generally inserts the new into an established pattern. Real rock is always a rebellion, always a disrespect to the hierarchy, a blow to the empire. The authentic article is never the commercial article. (23)

To the extent that Napster wished to participate in rock's stance, it was precluded from full partnership with the record industry because such an alliance would have violated the company's established ethos.

Its fans developed a particularly strong affinity for Napster because Fanning had internalized the first generation of hackers' focus on community-building and embedded it in the Napster software. Indeed, in Fanning we can see a blend of the expansive community-building advocated by Stallman, and the more materially-focused community organizations facilitated by the music traders who gathered on the WELL. Thus, while Fanning belonged demographically to a generation of geeks that would be criticized as "crackers," his software arguably exemplified the more idealistic principles of early hackers. Fanning's emphasis on the community-building potential of Napster is consistent and dates back to the company's inception. In a 2000 interview, Fanning said:

> I was at Northeastern University playing with the idea and getting feedback from my roommates, and then started drafting a really basic design idea. It was rooted out of frustration not only with mp3.com, Lycos, and Scour.net, but also to create a music community. There really was nothing like it at the time. (Varanini)

And indeed, Fanning's software represented an important step forward from other services cataloging and delivering MP3 music files, Napster allowed for direct communication among users of the Napster software, so an individual downloading a particular song might well receive an instant message from the person serving that song to the network. Napster consistently spotlighted this feature. Napster's press releases included a boilerplate phrase claiming that Napster "provide[d] media fans a forum to communicate their interests and tastes with one another."

The company seized on this functionality when music copyright holders like the band Metallica began complaining about the alleged theft of their intellectual property via Napster's network. Napster's first CEO, Eileen Richardson, attempted to maintain a posture of corporate responsibility when she repurposed Shawn Fanning's "community" theme. Richardson said: "It's about community. Maybe I know about this band just in our local town, and you know about them, too. I can share that with you directly. It's not about known artists like Madonna" (qtd. in Menn, 226). Richardson was attempting to focus attention on one of Napster's potentially non-infringing uses: the sharing of unsigned bands among tiny circles of fans. But at the same time, Napster's website stated that Napster "ensures the availability of every song online" and further, that Napster "virtually guarantees you'll find the song you want when you want it [. . .] and you can forget about wading through page after page of unknown artists." This implicit invitation to what the major labels describe as piracy and theft suggests that Napster's ethos was not grounded in assertions of virtue, but rather in something like Kenneth Burke's identification, which Burke explains most clearly in *A Rhetoric of Motives:*

> *A* is not identical with his colleague, *B*. But insofar as their interests are joined, *A* is *identified* with *B*. Or he may *identify himself* with *B* even when their interests are not joined, if he assumes that they are, or is persuaded

> to believe so. Two persons may be identified in terms of some principle they share in common, an *identification* that does not deny their distinctness. To identify *A* with *B* is to make *A consubstantial* with *B*. (20-21)

Burkean identification offers rhetor and audience the opportunity to unite over a shared principle without necessarily verifying the virtue of either party. Thus, by maintaining the music-loving hacker Shawn Fanning as the public face of Napster, the company promoted an identification with fans of rock and hip-hop music that maintained the anti-corporate, anti-authoritarian stance of those musical genres. This proved especially damaging when the debate shifted from a public relations battle between Napster and the Recording Industry Association of America to a pointedly legal battle between Napster on one side and Metallica and Dr. Dre on the other.

Metallica describes itself as the "7th biggest selling act in American history." The band's success is grounded in a close relationship with its fan base—so close that when Metallica's members collectively updated their hairstyles, the act was seen as a capitulation to the image-consciousness promoted by MTV, but at odds with Metallica's anti-corporate ethos. Metallica's lyrics, too, position the band as vocal critics of a vaguely constructed network of authority figures, including record companies, parents, and the U.S. government, a critique which is expressed most directly on the band's album, ". . . And Justice for All," which features the iconic figure of Lady Justice being toppled by four ropes (probably corresponding to the four band members). The title song's lyrics also bespeak a frustration with the degree to which "power wolves" pollute the justice system with money and influence.

A similarly oppositional stance, albeit one arising from a different space within U.S. culture, is everywhere apparent in Dr. Dre's work. Dre's career can be traced back to his membership in the Los Angeles-based group Niggaz With Attitude, whose breakout single, "Fuck Tha Police," was a withering indictment of the Los Angeles Police Department's racist practices, and this critique predated Rodney King and the L.A. riots. A producer, writer, and performer—whom *Rolling Stone* has compared to both Phil Spector, the architect of the 1960s "Wall of Sound," and Quincy Jones, the producer of the biggest-selling record of all time—Dre has crafted an identity that balances his success as a performer and entrepreneur with the markers of "street credibility" that allow him to maintain a productive identification with his audience. Thus, while Dre was the owner of a record label, the label was named "Death Row Records," associating his work with the politics of capital punishment, a practice that the State of Illinois suspended in 2000 due to its evidently racist application. In the lyrics to his 1999 rap, "Forgot About Dre," Dre also somewhat disingenuously positioned himself as a struggling small business owner, refusing handouts because his company is too "little" and because he is too street-smart to be taken advantage of.

Once Dre and Metallica entered the legal arena, the Recording Industry Association of America backed away from its aggressive attempts to set the terms of the Napster debate, relying instead on the sometimes inarticulate voices of Metallica's drummer, Lars Ulrich, and Dr. Dre to carry the industry's arguments to the public. At times, this undoubtedly proved excruciating for the industry. In one interview, Ulrich compared Napster's claim that it could not hope to control whether the technology's users violated copyrights or not as the equivalent of the National Rifle Association's infamous "Guns Don't Kill People, People Do," argument. While Ulrich is correct in pointing to a superficial similarity between the arguments, the comparison also tacitly equates copyright infringement with murder. Clearly, this is not an optimal rhetorical presentation. Ulrich's Senate testimony was widely criticized by the band's fans as a betrayal; indeed, the juxtaposition of "Mr. Lars Ulrich" with the gentle questioning of Senator Orrin Hatch was one of the more irresistible pop culture mind grenades since Elvis shook hands with Richard Nixon, and a direct violation of Ulrich's then settled image as a rock and roll wildman.

And while Dre is verbally inventive as a writer and performer, his public statements on Napster were disappointingly brief and vague. His most direct public engagement with Napster came in a press release wherein he stated, baldly "I don't like people stealing my music," without addressing the complex questions arising from peer-to-peer technologies (Dansby). Dre's participation in the argument was further complicated by his position as a hip-hop producer who had made extensive use of sampling technology on his records, sometimes with permission but often without. In fact, at the time of the lawsuit, Dre himself was being sued by George Lucas for having sampled the "Dolby THX" sound that precedes some films, without first securing permission. And given that the sound was followed by a barrage of bong hits and profanity, it seems clear that Lucas, as a family-friendly entrepreneur would have denied permission.

Nevertheless, the industry hung back, allowing Ulrich, in particular, to function in the role of the aggrieved artist, and by so doing the industry transformed the Napster argument from a likely loser into an argument powerful enough to persuade a crucial district court judge to enjoin file-transfers via Napster's site. Because Metallica and Dre so fully inhabited an outlaw ethos which allied them with fans and against the same authoritarian, corporate architecture which Napster had targeted, the industry succeeded in creating uncertainty and debate within a fan base that, prior to Metallica's and Dre's entering the argument, was united behind Napster's implied assertions that music ought to be free.

Thus, while Napster initially offered a viable alternative to business as usual within the music industry by crafting an ethos that paralleled rock's and hip-hop's superficial rejection of authority and corporate politics, this ethos left Napster with only limited opportunities to reposition itself as a legitimate business. When, in the midst of this process, it faced a challenge from the very performers who had inspired its existence, Napster faced an argument it could not win without "selling out." In the music industry, this is a familiar narrative. Like many performers in its favored genres, Napster failed to successfully negotiate the difficult task of preserving its projected authenticity and integrity when the company became an "overnight sensation." But this is not the sort of narrative that ought to lie at the heart of an important discussion about public policy. Napster was allowed to function as a representative for *all* peer-to-peer applications and networks, and its eventual defeat created a circumstance in which even clearly legal uses of peer-to-peer technologies are now greeted with wariness (especially by university attorneys who are compelled to err on the side of caution).

Ironically, Fanning was a big fan of both of the most prominent music acts to pursue litigation against Napster. In the wake of the commencement of Metallica's litigation against Napster, Fanning made a particular point of stressing his enjoyment of Metallica's music, even appearing on an MTV award program wearing a Metallica t-shirt. Napster depended on Fanning's public persona to forge a link to the communities of music fans he superficially represented, but this dependence carried with it a lingering association with the now marginalized and suspect practice of hacking.

In its review of Joseph Menn's history of the brief life and death of Napster 1.0, the *New York Times* refers to "Mr. Fanning, the *wunderkind* hacker who invented Napster when he was just a college student." In so doing, the *Times* contributes to the increasingly fixed portrait of Fanning as a member of what Ross described as the "deviant social class" of "teenage hackers." Because Napster persists as the emblematic example of a peer-to-peer network among members of the general public, this inaccurate presentation of Fanning as more cracker than hacker is also perpetuated. The ultimate consequence is that it is now common for legislators and members of the lay public to misconstrue the *whole* of peer-to-peer file transfers—a staple phenomenon within the Internet—as an expression of hackers' characteristic transgressions against traditional property lines.

3 The Positioning of Peer-to-Peer Transfers as Theft

In the mid 1960s, Lyman Ray Patterson undertook the challenging project of revisiting the often-arcane machinations surrounding early British laws addressing copyrights and "literary property." Patterson hoped to use historical analysis to reveal "aspects of law which logical analysis does not bring into focus" (v). Patterson pursued path-breaking work on the early history of copyright, but he did so always with an eye toward understanding and explaining the particularities of his own historical circumstance. Fortuitously, Patterson's book arrived one year prior to the first stirrings of the Internet, so it offers a snapshot of arguments embedded in a culture rich in media opportunities but free from the particular challenges that would later be presented by digital media. Patterson closes his book by articulating three principles that he deems "necessary for an integrated concept of copyright" (228). Taken together, Patterson's principles constitute a sharp and prescient critique of the general arc of copyright policy in the latter half of the twentieth century. Patterson writes:

1. [A] copyright owner has a right against an economic competitor to the exclusive reproduction in its original or derivative form.
2. [A]n author retains an inalienable right to protect the integrity of his work, and his reputation in connection therewith.
3. [T]he right of individuals to the use of copyrighted work for personal, private, or reasonable uses shall not be impaired. (228)

Patterson's first principle is directed at limiting the scope of copyright infringement to those instances where the economic interests of the copyright owner are clearly affected. Patterson refers to this as "protecting the entrepreneur, not the work itself," and argues that: "the basic function of copyright is to protect the publisher—not against the author or individual user, but against other publishers" (228). Patterson's second principle accords rights to the author that had been subsumed, under U.S. copyright law, by publishers. This principle would, in practice, allow an author to pursue damages against a publisher who failed to accurately reproduce the author's work. It contrasts with contemporary practice in which an author would have little recourse after the point at which her copyright had been transferred to a publisher. Patterson's third principle, however, represents the most radical challenge to copyright "business as usual." Structurally, the third principle corresponds closely with the U.S. Constitution's second Amendment. If Patterson meant to invite this comparison, the suggestion is that because the U.S. acknowledges a right to "private," "personal," and "reasonable" uses of *weaponry,* the comparatively mild questions of whether individuals may go about their business with loaded or concealed copyrights should also be easily and definitively settled. While Patterson's persistent focus is on the relationship between copyright policy and freedom of expression, here his emphasis falls on citizens' expectations of privacy. While Patterson wholeheartedly endorses copyright's role in protecting publishers from piracy, he would allow no intrusions into private and personal consumption of copyrighted materials.

Patterson's principles predate the popular adoption of digital media, but his arguments are nevertheless informed by his attentiveness to the copying technologies available at the time he wrote. In a critical paragraph, Patterson suggests that the advent of a particular copying technology has prompted an over-reaching response by copyright holders:

> The limited ability of the individual a few years ago to reproduce a book has been changed by the availability of high-speed copying machines. The change has made copyright owners—that is, publishers—look to the long-continued concept of monopoly in the guise of property rights to protect their interest. A more subtle and significant point is overlooked. However slight the danger, the failure to recognize the individual user's right results in a limitation upon the freedom of expression. The copyright owner's complete control of the work, based on the notion of

> the expression of ideas for profit, allows him to control that work completely. (227–28)

Though the World Intellectual Property Organization (WIPO) was founded in 1967, at the time Patterson wrote, it was not yet common practice to refer to patents, trademarks, and copyrights as "intellectual property." Patterson here rejects the implicit analogy, suggested by invocations of property, arguing that the "guise of property rights" is a euphemistic substitution for the less-palatable "monopoly." Because the copyright monopoly mandated by the Constitution is, in practice, transferred efficiently and wholly from creators to publishers, the scope and reach of copyright have expanded exponentially. Patterson's principles foreshadow the degree to which the expansion of copyright law would impinge on the personal and private uses of copyrighted material that U.S. citizens once took for granted.

One of the first books to wrestle with the ramifications of digital media for copyright law was Paul Goldstein's *Copyright's Highway: The Law and Lore of Copyright from Gutenberg to the Celestial Jukebox*. Published in 1994, *Copyright's Highway* features an attempt to toe Patterson's lines that is marked (and marred) by hedged language:

> Every American copyright act since 1790 has clung to the idea that copyright is a law of public places and commercial interests—retail sales of books, public performances if plays or movies, radio or television broadcasts of every kind of performance. This idea has dominated some of copyright law's central doctrines: only public, not private performances infringe copyright; noncommercial uses are more likely to be held fair use than commercial ones; to prevail against a fair use defense, a copyright holder must often show that it has suffered economic harm. (131)

The first sentence in this excerpt is satisfyingly absolutist, and the casting of copyright as directed at the public and the commercial matches up very well with Patterson's first and third principles. The second sentence, by contrast, is littered with exceptions and limitations. Goldstein's enumeration of "central doctrines" starts with a promising emphasis on public performance as a requirement for infringement. But in stating that noncommercial uses are "more likely" to be considered fair use than commercial uses, Goldstein isteps back from Patterson's principles and leaving open the possibility that noncommercial uses *might not* be considered fair use, and thus infringe. And in the final clause, Goldstein suggests that demonstration of economic harm is not an absolute requirement for a copyright holder alleging infringement.

The gap between Patterson's principles and Goldstein's account of contemporary copyright in operation is significant. While Patterson called for sharp limits on publishers' ability to pursue cases of infringement in the absence of public performance/sale and demonstrable economic harm, Goldstein, surveying 1994's newly networked environment, must acknowledge that Patterson's calls are being drowned out by increasingly aggressive copyright enforcement. Goldstein's language—however grudgingly—acknowledges that copyright holders were successfully pursuing cases where no public performance or sale had occurred, and where no demonstrable economic harm could be established.

In the years since Goldstein's assessment, there has been a dramatic expansion in the amount of control ceded to U.S. copyright holders. And when I say "ceded," I mean to stress that in a U.S. context, copyrights are granted by the public, via Congress, to copyright holders. The Constitution specifies that "Congress shall have the power [. . .] to promote the progress of science and useful arts, by securing for limited times to authors and inventors the exclusive right to their respective writings and discoveries." Thus, in the United States, the foundational intellectual property protections (copyrights and patents) are offered by the people, via Congress, as an incentive for further production from authors and inventors. This represents a subtle but significant break from a broader European tradition in which the so-called "natural rights" of the author or inventor function as the basis for intellectual property protections. This distinction is, in part, why for many years the U.S. maintained a sharp gap between penalties for infringement (monetary damages adjudicated in civil court) and theft (imprisonment adjudicated by criminal courts). In this now lost context, economic penalties for infringement were appropriate because infringers introduced inefficiencies into or disrupted markets for copyrighted materials. Infringers harmed publishers and ultimately the public because they diminished incentives for progress in science and useful arts. By contrast, criminal penalties were inappropriate because copyright law was focused on the public's access to the maximum output from creators, and *not* on addressing injuries to individual creators (whereas under a moral rights regime the injury to the creator's reputation and interests would be critical). And this understanding arguably persisted from 1790 until the No Electronic Theft (NET) Act of 1997.

Prior to 1997, there were a few statutes on the books specifying criminal penalties for copyright infringement, but these statutes were all directed at activities that could fairly be described as public sale or performance, obviously causing direct economic harm, like the 1897 statute forbidding unauthorized public performances of plays and musical compositions. The NET Act, by contrast, represents the point at which infringements that might never travel beyond private and personal use—the uses Patterson wished to place beyond copyright's reach—became felonies and misdemeanors. The NET Act begins by altering a passage in the U.S. Code which read: "(a) Criminal Infringement.—Any person who infringes a copyright willfully and for purposes of commercial advantage or private financial gain shall be punished [. . .]." This statutory language embedded a Pattersonian emphasis on measurable economic harm into copyright policy, which the NET Act no longer requires. The NET Act, through a subtle relocation of a crucial clause, dramatically expands the scope of criminal infringement.

§ 506. Criminal offenses

(a) Criminal Infringement—Any person who infringes a copyright willfully
1 for purposes of commercial advantage or private financial gain, or
2. by the reproduction or distribution, including by electronic means, during any 180-day period, of 1 or more copies or phonorecords of 1 or more copyrighted works, which have a total retail value of more than $1,000, shall be punished as provided under section 2319 of title 18.

The revised statute thus repositions "for-profit" infringement as one of two roughly equivalent types of criminally infringing activity. The second class of infringements includes not only distribution but mere "reproduction" of copyrighted materials. To date, the bulk of the convictions under the NET Act have involved substantial distributions of computer software, but, in one case, a man was prosecuted for making a single film (*Star Wars Episode 1: The Phantom Menace*) available to others on his website. While this individual used exceedingly poor judgment in choosing to redistribute the whole of a high profile film, then still in theatrical release, via his own personal webspace, the fact that he was successfully prosecuted under the NET Act for a single infringement illustrates the degree to which the NET Act has lowered the bar. Under the NET Act, it is now theoretically possible for a person who possesses (but does not distribute or circulate) a single infringing theatrical release to face imprisonment for up to one year, and a fine of up to $100,000. And this does not preclude the possibility of additional civil action against the infringer. More troublingly, the NET Act implies that even without distribution, the *reproduction* of copyrighted materials is the equivalent of "theft." Even though it isn't.

At this point, I am obliged to stress that I am not a lawyer, and that this text ought not be understood as a substitute for legal advice from a trained and certified professional, but there are many instances when the reproduction of even a heavily commercialized piece of copyrighted material would be found—if not legal—at least well below the threshold at which a court would or should consent to hear the matter. This is not to say that the majority of the uses of Napster were clearly legal, or that the majority of uses of contemporary peer-to-peer networks are clearly legal, but it *is* to say that the mere act of reproducing copyrighted material or of securing copies of copyrighted material via peer-to-peer networks ought not, in and of itself, be regarded as the equivalent of theft.

If, for example, a classroom instructor downloaded a copy of rapper Eminem's virulently sexist "My Dad's Gone Crazy" in order to critique the rapper's decision to involve his daughter in the recording, or to interrogate Eminem's description of himself as "Clyde" to his daughter's "Bonnie," this use would almost certainly be found to be a fair use. Let's assume that, as a point of principle, the instructor does not wish to support Eminem or his record company in any way, and so the instructor's decision to download the file is grounded in a pointed refusal to compensate the copyright holders for art that he views as distasteful. Even though the instructor's use is arguably a substitution for a purchase, the instructor's download of the Eminem track almost certainly passes the four point "fair use test."

The *purpose* of the use is expressly non-commercial and educational. Courts have historically granted special consideration to uses in furtherance of education, and it is clear the instructor is not benefiting financially from the use. The *nature* of the copyrighted work is heavily commercial, which argues against the instructor's use being judged "fair." The *amount* of the song used by the instructor is, in this hypothetical, the entire song. While elements of the song make it a questionable choice for even a graduate seminar, let's assume the instructor was bold and allowed students to confront the whole of the roughly five-minute recording. This, too, argues against a determination of fair use. The *effect* of the use on the market for the copyrighted work is, for all practical purposes, nil. Here, the instructor is on *extremely* solid footing. The in-class performance has no plausible impact on the market for Eminem's music. While some might be persuaded by the terms of the instructor's criticism to rethink purchases they were planning, others might conclude that the charge of sexism is outweighed by other considerations, or that the song simply sounded really cool. Thus, while the instructor's download and performance involves the reproduction and circulation (albeit ephemerally) of the whole of a heavily commercialized product, the context, wherein the work was serving as an object of criticism within an educational institution, outweighs any concerns that the use might otherwise raise.

Because the first U.S. Copyright Act is entitled "An Act for the Encouragement of Learning," all parties to the peer-to-peer debates have a special obligation to acknowledge that people do and should download cultural artifacts for legitimate educational purposes. When these uses meet the standards established by the codification of fair use, *they are legal*. Or at least, *probably* legal. Ultimately, the legality or illegality of any particular use would hinge on the determination of a judge or panel of judges in a given geographic subsection of the United States. And the interpretation of copyright law has proven highly variable depending on the district in which potential litigants reside. But this variability is not, ultimately, the fault of the courts, as U.S. federal legislators have refused to offer "bright line" distinctions, preferring instead for judges to make the kinds of fine-grained decisions called for in copyright cases. In the absence of case law addressing a precisely parallel circumstance, copyright consumers are routinely left to guess whether their uses are legal. Of course, the absence of clear markers means, in practical terms, that those wishing to use material that *might* be protected by copyright must err on the side of caution or assume some measure of risk of litigation. In the future, it may become technically feasible to monitor, track, and evaluate many, if not all, uses of copyrighted material. But few consumers of copyrighted material would exchange our current and admittedly confusing circumstance for one in which the boundaries were both clear and readily enforceable.

This is especially true because virtually *everything* virtual is copyrighted. Because the U.S. has eliminated requirements for notice and registration, the default status for any finished artifact of expression is that it is copyrighted. The sole requirement for a work to be considered copyrighted is *fixity*. All of the e-mails that have ever been sent are "fixed" enough for purposes of copyright. Every Web page is, similarly "fixed." Those of us whose workdays involve significant use of the Internet spend our days constantly reproducing copyrighted material. Given the low economic value of most e-mail messages and websites, the threat of litigation over these potential infringements is low, but it is not absent. If, as the NET Act suggests, "reproduction" of copyrighted material constitutes "theft," then we are all thieves.

Sadly, this government endorsement of an expansive characterization of "theft" emboldened the content industries, who responded to Napster with a coordinated campaign directed at ensuring that digital downloads would not be understood in their challenging complexity. Representatives of the recording industry consistently characterized downloads as theft. A March, 2000, *Time* magazine story features an especially hyperbolic example of the kind of rhetoric emanating from the RIAA and its constituents, along with some surprisingly tart editorializing from writer Karl Taro Greenfeld:

> "Napster is the greatest example of aiding and abetting a theft that I have ever seen," says Ron Stone, manager of Bonnie Raitt and Tracy Chapman, among other artists. "Ninety-nine percent of their content is illegal." What really bothers Stone and the rest of the biz is the fact that 100% of their content is free—no money for the labels, artists or managers. ("Free")

The RIAA encouraged prominent musicians to perpetuate analogy between digital downloading and physical theft. By 2001, the RIAA's website was soon filled with brief statements like this one from Creed lead singer Scott Stapp:

> The day I decided to share my music with the world, was the day I decided to walk the fine line between art and commerce. I have been blessed in that I do what I love and can support my family with what I create. When my music is given away, as taboo as it is for me to say, it is stealing. I need not defend my motives for making music, but the distribution of my music has made me business conscious. I have decided to sell my music to anyone who wants it, that is how I feed my family, just like a doctor, lawyer, judge, or teacher. Not to insult anyone's intelligence, but my music is like my home. Napster is sneaking in the back door and robbing me blind. (Stapp)

While there are obvious distinctions to be drawn between real/physical and intellectual/virtual properties, the RIAA took steps to ensure that peer-to-peer downloads were consistently judged according to the rules established to address property in physical spaces.

The apotheosis of the RIAA's efforts to equate Napster-enabled digital downloading with physical theft occurred during Metallica drummer Lars Ulrich's July 2000 Senate testimony:

> If you're not fortunate enough to own a computer, there's only one way to assemble a music collection the equivalent of a Napster user's: theft. Walk into a record store, grab what you want and walk out. The difference is that the familiar phrase a computer user hears, "File's done," is replaced by another familiar phrase, "You're under arrest." (Ulrich)

This argument hinges on the flat equation of physical artifacts (CDs) and readily reproducible digital files (MP3s). In Ulrich's hypothetical, the record store owner is harmed by the loss of an existing investment in the compact discs, in anticipation of their eventual sale. In the absence of the physical copies, the retailer has no way to recoup that investment. The loss of tangible property (CDs) results in a tangible financial loss.

By contrast, in the case of a downloaded file, the uploader and downloader each retain perfect copies. There is net *gain* in the amount of property available. While the harm to retailers is clear in cases of physical theft, the harm caused by digital downloads is difficult to quantify. Though the RIAA has argued vociferously that each download is tantamount to a lost sale, the truth is much more complex. Some peer-to-peer users describe their downloading as "sampling" and claim to purchase retail copies of the music they enjoy. Others are clearly downloading files because once the fees for Internet service are paid, the downloads are "free." Whether they would in fact be purchasing the songs they download in the absence of this "free" option is impossible to know, but reason suggests that only a fraction of the downloaded songs would prompt purchases. Even the aggregate effect of unauthorized peer-to-peer downloads on music sales is uncertain. A 2004 economic analysis by Felix Oberholzer of the Harvard Business School and Koleman Strumpf of the University of North Carolina arrived at a surprising conclusion:

> We find that file sharing has no statistically significant effect on purchases of the average album in our sample. Moreover, the estimates are of rather modest size when compared to the drastic reduction in sales in the music industry. At most, file sharing can explain a tiny fraction of this decline. This result is plausible given that movies, software, and video games are actively downloaded, and yet these industries have continued to grow since the advent of file sharing.

But even if the casting of peer-to-peer downloading as "theft" ultimately does not map neatly in terms of demonstrable physical harm, the characterization still has rhetorical power, as the RIAA surely understood.

The charge of theft, especially when paired with an idealized presentation of copyright, constitutes a powerful *pathos* appeal, grounded in the notion that the author has worked hard and expended effort and deserves to be rewarded for this expenditure. Ulrich's testimony underscores this point:

> Since what I do is make music, let's talk about the recording artist for a moment. When Metallica makes an album we spend many months and many hundreds of thousands of our own dollars writing and recording. We also contribute our inspiration and perspiration. It's what we do for a living. Even though we're passionate about it, it's our job. (Ulrich)

But copyright makes no allowance for inspiration and perspiration. Indeed, the law makes no distinction between the by-products of Metallica's "job" and a recording like Jimi Hendrix's "Band of Gypsies," which documents a live performance on New Year's Eve, 1970. While Hendrix's inspiration and perspiration were certainly involved, they would have been present even if this performance had not been recorded.

U.S. courts have repeatedly rejected the notion that the creators of intellectual property are entitled to any special consideration based on their investment of labor. As recently as 1991, the U.S. Supreme Court expressly rejected the idea of "natural rights" arising from "sweat of the brow." In *Feist v. Rural Telephone Service,* a phone book publisher sued for copyright infringement when the specific arrangement of names and numbers in its "white pages" was reproduced without permission by a competitor. Writing for the majority, Justice Sandra Day O'Connor was careful to emphasize that the public's interest in access to information can trump the creators' expectation for a return on effort expended, writing:

> It may seem unfair that much of the fruit of the compiler's labor may be used by others without compensation. As Justice Brennan has correctly observed, however, this is not "some unforeseen byproduct of a statutory scheme." [. . .] It is, rather, "the essence of copyright," and a constitutional requirement. The primary objective of copyright is not to reward the labor of authors, but "[t]o promote the Progress of Science and useful Arts." To this end, copyright assures authors the right to their original expression, but encourages others to build freely upon the ideas and information conveyed by a work. (*Feist*)

Seven justices joined O'Connor in this opinion and Justice Harry Blackmun concurred, creating, in effect, a unanimous endorsement of the principles O'Connor articulates here. For its first two centuries, U.S. copyright law was commonly understood as emphasizing the public benefit of *progress* even if this interpretation at times required failing to acknowledge considerable labor. It is difficult—perhaps even impossible—to reconcile the strong bias toward public access articulated in *Feist* with many of the laws and legal decisions that materialized in its wake.

A decade after *Feist,* the U.S. District Court for the Northern District of California issued a ruling that ended Napster's reign as the most popular "free" peer-to-peer application. Though the RIAA routinely characterized Napster's activities as "theft," it is important to recognize that Napster never housed MP3 files on its servers. Rather, Napster's servers housed a comprehensive index of the locations of MP3 files on Napster users' computers. To return to Lars Ulrich's record store analogy, it was never Napster itself that was "grabbing" copies of copyrighted material. Rather, Napster was alerting its users to the locations where *they* could set about grabbing. Except, as discussed, the "grabbing" was not from a "record store owner" but from other Napster users and the "grabbing" ultimately produced more copies of the works in question.

Nevertheless, as the Napster case wended through the courts, the company was directed to eliminate the indexing information for copyrighted material from its servers. Judge Marilyn Hall Patel's March 2001 injunction had required Napster to purge music files within three days of being notified that the files were subject to an actively managed copyright. If Napster maintained a copyrighted file beyond that point, the court's holding was that Napster was guilty of contributory infringement. In July of 2001, Napster reported that it had blocked the indexing of 99.4% of the files identified by copyright holders. A Napster attorney stated that the music industry, in its own canvas of music indexed on Napster's servers, located pointers to only 174 prospectively infringing files out of 950,000 index entries (or .02 percent). Napster argued that these figures indicated that the company was in substantial compliance with the judge's order. A contemporaneous article from C/NET's news.com service reports that Judge Marilyn Hall Patel did not find this claim persuasive:

> [M]usic industry attorney Russell Frackman told Patel that just one unauthorized song on the system could have deleterious effects on an artist because it could be distributed to millions of people. "The law does not tolerate any infringement," he said.
>
> Patel agreed, saying she would have a zero tolerance policy for swapping. "There should be no copyright infringement, period," Patel said.
>
> When Napster attorneys asked Patel for a standard that would allow them to go back online, Patel replied, "the standard is to get it down to zero, do you understand that?" (Hansen and Bowman)

In fact, the law *does* tolerate infringement, or it least it did for many years. Many Napster advocates cited the 1984 Supreme Court ruling in the so-called *Betamax* case as supporting their right to make and keep non-commercial copies of songs for their personal use. In this case, Universal Studios sued Sony for having marketed a home videotape recorder—a VCR—alleging that the primary use of the VCR as a technology was the enabling of piracy, and that Sony should be held liable for contributory infringement. While the court acknowledged the likelihood of VCR owners archiving copies of copyrighted films and programs, the Court also recognized that the VCR had a significant non-infringing use: the recording of programs for viewing at a later date, or time-shifting, and it ruled in favor of this non-infringing use without directly addressing the problem of archived videotapes harming the markets for commercial releases of copyrighted material.

The question of whether individual consumers can legally record and preserve copyrighted materials for personal use was also addressed by the Audio Home Recording Act of 1991. This Act protects manufacturers of recording devices from the charge that their devices were enabling contributory infringement when home users violated copyrights. (In this case, the technology driving the law was Digital Audio Tape or DAT.) But this protection came with a price. Manufacturers of DAT players and DAT tapes were also obliged to pay fees designed to address the likelihood that purchasers of DAT tape would be using this high quality recording medium as a substitute for commercially produced recordings. Unlike the VCR, the DAT was never meant to time-shift broadcasted material—its chief purpose was creating the best possible reproductions of previously recorded material. Nevertheless, the legislative history found in the house reports leading to the Audio Home Recording Act makes it clear that, at least at that time, home recording for private, non-commercial use was not being targeted. This is most apparent in a passage which reads: "In short, the reported legislation would clearly establish that consumers cannot be sued for making analog or digital audio copies for private noncommercial use." (qtd. in Carroll, 1993)

The general import of both the Audio Home Recording Act *and* the holding in the *Betamax* case is that technologies facilitating both infringing and non-infringing copying ought not be withheld from the public, *even if the availability of the technologies leads to infringing uses.* And while Congress offered special compensation to copyright holders for anticipated infringements by DAT users, the Supreme Court offered no such compensation to copyright holders for the expected infringements by home videotapers. If we follow the logic of these policy decisions, it seems clear that the peer-to-peer file transfer system at the heart of Napster, *if understood as a technology,* ought to have remained available to the public because, like the VCR, the technology is capable of substantial non-infringing uses. The only real question should have been whether, like DAT, Napster and the machines associated with it ought to be subject to fees that would have been distributed to copyright holders as compensation for anticipated infringements. As with the VCR, Napster users employed this peer-to-peer technology for a variety of purposes, many of which are certainly no more problematic than a Betamax tape housing a recording of one of HBO's screenings of *Risky Business*. But Napster and its lawyers were unable to build a persuasive case for the range of uses common in peer-to-peer environments. This is in part because Napster limited its scope to music files. While this focus enhanced Napster's functionality, it also curtailed Napster's ability to claim that the technology was suitable for general circulation of media files.

In addition to the general fair use defenses that would arguably insulate certain downloaders of files from charges of infringement, there are also uses that, while technically infringing on a copyright, are nevertheless unworthy of the expenditure of time and money associated with a court proceeding. Copyright jurisprudence has a long history of invoking the *de minimis* doctrine, drawn from the Latin expression *de minimis non curant lex*, which is commonly translated as "the law does not concern itself with trifles."

Many such "trifling" infringements were arguably at the heart of Napster's popularity. In many cases, users valued Napster not because it offered access to copies of the Top-40 hits of the fortnight, but because it offered the only available avenue for distributing digital recordings of music that had long ago exhausted their viability in the compact disc marketplace. For example, for reasons best left for readers to speculate about, I enjoy the music of Davie Allan and the Arrows, a band best known for their contributions to the soundtrack of "The Wild Angels," a 1966 film starring Peter Fonda and Nancy Sinatra. I feel fortunate to own the two vinyl soundtrack LPs that were released at the time the film came out, which I located only after considerable time spent trolling the LP bins at flea markets and used record stores. These LPs are long out-of-print, hard to find, and collectible. And I would like to have a digital version of the albums. But I missed my opportunity. There was a CD release in 1996, but the CD is now out of print. There are no copies for sale on Amazon.com, and at least six buyers are now hoping for a copy to purchase. So if I now determine to listen to the songs from "The Wild Angels" on my iPod, I'll need to record the LPs to my hard drive, scrub the pops and clicks from the LP, label the tracks, and convert those recordings to MP3s. Commercial services charge in excess of $50 per record to perform this process, as it is fairly time-consuming and labor-intensive. It's also a process that really only *needs* to be performed once, if widespread access to peer-to-peer technologies is maintained.

When Napster was active, the first legitimate owner to rip digital files from an LP often posted them, and saved others the arduous step of recording and ripping those files. If I had been attentive to the opportunity, I might have downloaded the *Wild Angels* soundtrack music from Napster, and, given my legitimate ownership of the LPs, my possession of the MP3 versions of the music for personal use would, in a reasonable court, be found to be just the sort of "trifle" that ought not trigger a court proceeding. The problem, of course, is that digital media are hard to contain. The exchange of the *Wild Angels* tracks seems clearly *de minimis* when both the uploader and the downloader are legitimate purchasers of the songs, whatever the medium. But no peer-to-peer network to date has pursued a model that would limit participation to purchasers (though the my.mp3.com case addressed in the impending "Piracy" chapter offers a close approximation). The robustness of the networks is a direct function of the easy reproducibility of digital files. The networks depend on multiple copies radiating throughout the network. Thus, while *my* hypothetical download would arguably have been *de minimis,* there is also a strong chance that my ability to easily locate and download the *Wild Angels* files would depend on copies having been made and relayed among a fairly substantial pool of users, at least some of whom had never taken advantage of an opportunity to purchase the *Wild Angels* soundtrack music in any form.

The Napster debate, by spotlighting Lars Ulrich's specious arguments, served to perpetuate a fundamental misconception with respect to users of peer-to-peer technologies: that they are "thieves" of other people's "property." This perception remains dominant despite the absence of precise correspondences to physical theft and real property, as Vaidhyanathan points out:

> We make a grave mistake when we choose to engage in discussions of copyright in terms of "property." Copyright is not about "property" as commonly understood. It is a specific state-granted monopoly issued for particular policy reasons. While, technically, it describes real property as well, it also describes a more fundamental public good that precedes specific policy choices the state may make about the regulation and dispensation of property. But we can't win an argument as long as those who hold inordinate interest in copyright maximization can cry "theft" at any mention of fair use or users' rights. You can't argue for theft. ("Copyright as Cudgel")

Napster's failure to successfully articulate the degree to which it enabled non-infringing, *de minimis,* and fair uses of music files cemented the music industry's inscription of users of peer-to-peer technologies as at best suspect, and, at worst, thieves. This characterization has diminished opportunities for the general public to develop a more reflective portrait of peer-to-peer users which would include, among others the classroom instructors who keep their courses current by briefly referencing current artworks; the Usenet users who build communities around shared interest in particular cultural artifacts; and archivists, who are struggling to maintain whatever seems most compelling amidst the torrents of data now available via the Internet. Instead, the Napster case now functions as a cautionary tale that drives not only public policy, but also the increasingly cautious policies of corporations trafficking in music and media. This point can be clearly illustrated by reviewing the activities of Apple Computer as it adapted its business to accommodate computer users' voracious appetite for digital music.

Figure 4. Apple's "Rip. Mix. Burn." campaign. Copyright © 2001, Apple Computer, Inc.

In February of 2001, Apple Computer introduced a revision of its popular iMac computer with a feature customers had long sought: an onboard CD-RW drive. This was the first Macintosh machine to feature the ability not merely to read CD-ROMs and compact discs, but also to write discs filled with data or music. Apple chose to introduce this new feature with an ad campaign structured around the phrase "Rip. Mix. Burn." The slogan was understood by many as an invitation to copy data without permission. At a Spring 2002 hearing of the Senate Commerce Committee Michael Eisner, then CEO of Disney, testified that by using this phrase, Apple was informing prospective customers "that they can create a theft if they buy this computer. (Boliek)

Figure 5. A first-generation iPod bearing the "Don't Steal Music" sticker. Copyright © 2001, Mike Cohen.

In late 2001, as the complaints about the "Rip. Mix. Burn." campaign were mounting, Apple launched the iPod digital audio player. Purchasers who paid the $399 price for the five gigabyte iPod received an elegantly designed MP3 player (examples are now common in the industrial design sections of art museums). But the elegance of the design was undercut by a sticker affixed to the iPod's tiny LCD display. The sticker featured the phrase "Don't steal music" in four languages.

The directive, commanding tone is unusual for Apple, and indeed for most companies seeking to preserve a positive relationship with its customer base. In fairness, the German translation adds, *bitte,* ("please") to the injunction, but even in this form, the iPod remains that rare sort of product that greets its purchasers with an implied accusation. We would do well to understand how Apple moved from a rhetorical stance that was widely understood as providing a winking acknowledgment of consumers' potentially illicit consumption of music files to the marginally insulting assumption that iPod purchasers would steal unless told not to. As it turns out, Apple's contrasting rhetorical appeals fall neatly within the few months before and after the July 2001 shutdown of Napster.

Apple's "Rip. Mix. Burn." slogan was really more innocuous than it initially appeared. Computer terminology often sounds more violent and disruptive than it really is. For reasons that are, if not inscrutable, then at least beyond the scope of this project, computer jargon is littered with "slashes," "dumps," "hacks," and the like. The terms invoked by Apple all have fairly innocuous meanings within the context of the computing subculture. "Ripping" is simply the relocation of data from one storage medium to another. "Mixing" is not really a technical term at all. Here, Apple was drawing on the common practice of creating custom sequences of music, either in the form of cassette "mix tapes" or live mixes by disk jockeys on the radio or in the clubs. And "burning" is the practice of recording data in final form to (typically) a non-rewriteable disc. That said, the aggregate effect of these terms was clear. Apple was attempting to reach out to the population of music fans who had embraced Napster, and Apple's rhetorical positioning reflected the company's desire to lure fans of the genres favored by Napster's users, namely rock & roll and hip-hop.

There are practical reasons why both Napster and Apple targeted fans of these genres. Neither genre requires absolute musical fidelity, and thus both are especially amenable to circulation via MP3s. The MP3 compression format was initially developed to encode full-motion video in compact form for delivery on discs and over the Internet. For these purposes, MPEG-1 performs only acceptably. MPEG-1 is the basis for the Video CD format popular throughout Asia, but the image quality is comparable to VHS tapes, and obviously and visibly inferior to DVD images. The MPEG compression format delivered only marginal results with video, but it delivers much better results when its focus is limited to music.

While an MP3 file coded at the common rate of 128 bits per second would certainly not fool an audiophile, or even a trained ear, this rate delivers a listening experience very close to CD quality, especially when the genre involved is not predicated on the absence of distortion. Both rock and hip-hop are especially suited to MP3 distribution because the emotional impact of the music is usually more important to fans than the care with which it was recorded. Vaidhyanathan has pointed to both punk rock and hip-hop as genres that depended, for a time, on loose networks of fans circulating the music they loved on cassette tapes, with sound quality degrading noticeably each time a favorite record was dubbed (*Anarchist* 46).

While Apple could never acknowledge this directly, the iPod depended on peer-to-peer services like Napster to provide the "software" for its hardware. While it is technically a simple matter to rip files from CD to an iPod, it is also very time-consuming. In fact, in major cities, there are services like LoadPod, which charges $1.49 per CD to load music for iPod owners who do not wish to invest the considerable time needed to max out their iPods' storage. The initial five gigabyte iPod, released in 2001, could hold roughly 1,000 songs, or roughly ninety CDs worth of music. The current top-of-the-line iPod, at 80 gigabytes, holds roughly 20,000 songs, or over *1,600* CDs worth of music. Even assuming an optimistic fifteen minutes per ripped CD, an owner of the 80 gigabyte iPod could spend the better part of *seventeen* days, nonstop, loading CDs first into the computer, and then transferring them to the iPod. Admittedly, many users are taking advantage of the current iPod's video and photo storage abilities, and few choose to fill their iPods with music alone. But the ever-increasing storage capacity of the iPod (and its competitors) implicitly challenges the notion that most users are sitting around painstakingly loading music from their purchased CDs for days at a time.

By contrast, users of peer-to-peer services are able to quickly and efficiently load music into their portable players. The biggest bottleneck in the "ripping" process is the time it takes to transform the file from the relatively robust file size found on the compact disc, to the compressed file formats appropriate for digital audio players. Once this process has been completed, the file sizes are small enough that they are easily downloaded, transferred, and organized. Indeed, though it may seem counter-intuitive, many users of peer-to-peer networks download copies of songs they already own on vinyl LPs or CDs, simply because the speed with which they can achieve their goal of making a specific song portable greatly outstrips the time needed to accomplish the same task with their physical copies.

At the time the iPod was released, there were no stable and comprehensive commercial online music sources. Apple itself would not launch its own online music service, the iTunes Music Store, until April of 2003. Though Apple could not have fully anticipated Napster's closing at the time the iPod was developed, Apple almost certainly recognized that the success of the iPod hinged on the ready availability of music in the MP3 format (or a format very much like it) and thus must have implicitly understood that their product was thereby yoked to the continuing availability of peer-to-peer music downloads. A February 2001 ruling that complicated Napster's efforts to remain viable prompted a C/NET reporter to speculate that the increasing popularity of pre-iPod MP3 players was closely tethered to Napster's availability: "Despite shifts in consumers' perception of music and the popularity of MP3 players, there's no question that the closure of Napster would represent a big drain on MP3 player demand, even if only in the near term" (Konrad, "Makers"). The market for digital audio players like the iPod arose precisely because people had amassed large collections of music on their desktop computers and welcomed the opportunity to transfer those collections to more portable hardware. Without a steady supply of digital music files, the market for digital audio players would be sharply circumscribed. Even if robust commercial online music services had existed when the iPod launched, no reasonable person would imagine that the typical iPod user would be filling the device with music at prices like the $.99 per song or $9.99 per album eventually charged by Apple's iTunes music store. At these prices, the music within a fully loaded 60GB iPod would represent an expenditure of $8,000 to $10,000. Clearly, the iPod and the high-capacity MP3 players that compete with it are products whose utility depends upon low or no-cost downloads of music files.

But when Apple CEO Steve Jobs announced the launch of the iTunes Music Store in April 2003, he implicitly criticized many of the consumers who had purchased the iPod, and filled it with MP3s, from peer-to-peer services, especially Napster. Jobs touted the iTunes Music Store by saying, "It's not stealing, which is good karma" (Mainelli).

Thus, in the space of less than three years, Apple had moved from an advertising campaign that was widely understood as tacitly endorsing unauthorized copying of music, to suggesting that the majority of online music consumers were guilty of theft (and bad karma, to boot).

Whether or not Jobs ultimately believed in his characterization of peer-to-peer networks as facilitating "stealing" is less important than the context in which he spoke. By 2003, he could assert, without fear of significant reprisal, that Apple's commercial online music service offered an alternative to theft. And Jobs was able to make this claim because the Napster case, and the RIAA's associated campaigns against peer-to-peer technologies, had persuaded most Americans that the act of downloading copyrighted material from the Internet—whatever the context and purpose—was illegal. This victory was achieved in large part because of the successful rhetorical strategies of the content industries. And once these industries had persuaded Americans that downloading was criminal, the logical next step was to ensure that it was perceived as *violent* crime.

4 Peer-to-Peer Technologies as Piracy

In a lengthy July 26, 2000, hearing to determine whether the Napster peer-to-peer service ought to be shut down by an injunction while the merits of its case wended through the legal system, Ninth District Court Judge Marilyn Hall Patel was witheringly dismissive of Napster's attempts to present itself as an increasingly responsible corporation. Patel sketched a portrait of Shawn Fanning and Napster's developers that left little doubt as to how she would ultimately rule. Patel said, "This program was created to facilitate downloading, and pirating be damned." Later, Patel sharpened her critique, asserting that "Piracy was utmost in their minds; their thought was free music for the people" (Fitzpatrick). Napster was able to withstand the injunction Patel issued at the end of the 2000 hearing, but a year later, the company succumbed to a second injunction, and shut down its servers. And Napster's ultimate surrender had the unfortunate effect of perpetuating Patel's demonstrably false characterizations. The Recording Industry Association of America had, through its proxies, scored a tremendous victory.

This victory was not so much the legal jeopardy that had been visited upon a single peer-to-peer company as it was the Court's uncritical acceptance of "piracy" as an accurate description of Napster's activities. This usage radiated throughout media reports of the Napster lawsuits and embedded itself in the public's consciousness until it became difficult to recall that "piracy" had for many years had a specific and recognizable meaning well removed from the peer-to-peer downloads at the heart of the Napster case.

In *Digital Copyright,* law professor Jessica Litman offers a chapter entitled "Choosing Metaphors" in which she observes, "If you're dissatisfied with the way the spoils are getting divided, one approach is to change the rhetoric" (79). Litman goes on to present the content industries' repurposing of "piracy" as a signature example of a successful rhetorical shift:

> Piracy used to be about folks who made and sold large numbers of counterfeit copies. Today, the term "piracy" seems to describe *any* unlicensed activity—especially if the person engaging in it is a teenager. The content industry calls some behavior piracy despite the fact that it is unquestionably legal. When a consumer makes a noncommercial recording of music by, for example, taping a CD she has purchased or borrowed from a friend, her copying comes squarely within the privilege established by the Audio Home Recording Act. The record companies persist in calling that copying piracy even though the statute deems it lawful. (85)

Litman wrote this critique in 2001, and, since that time, the content industries have demonstrably embraced the positioning of Internet-driven peer-to-peer file transfers as piracy, as evidenced by a 2005 Web broadside by the RIAA entitled "Anti-Piracy":

> Online piracy is the unauthorized uploading of a copyrighted sound recording and making it available to the public, or downloading a sound recording from an Internet site, even if the recording isn't resold. Online piracy may now also include certain uses of "streaming" technologies from the Internet.

This presentation is dubious from a legal standpoint, but it clearly illustrates the degree to which the RIAA has embraced "piracy" as an all-encompassing term describing almost any unauthorized file transfer.

To properly recover a pre-Internet understanding of piracy I will resort to the hoary rhetorical strategy of offering and interpreting dictionary definitions. Though this may seem blisteringly obvious, it is important to note that the figurative uses of piracy are grounded in an analogic comparison to the activities of physical, nautical pirates. The term *pirate* is derived from an ancient Greek word meaning "to attempt, attack, or assault," and thus, the notion of theft *by force* or at least the threat of force is embedded into the term. This is reflected in the *Oxford English Dictionary*'s primary definition of *piracy* as "The practice or crime of robbery and depredation on the sea or navigable rivers [. . .] by persons not holding a commission from an established civilized state." Thus, maritime pirates are best understood as stateless predators who practice theft by force, or the threat of force. With this model in mind, I turn to the figurative uses of piracy.

The *OED*'s second definition of piracy reads as follows: "The appropriation and reproduction of an invention or work of another for one's own profit, without authority; infringement of the rights conferred by a patent or copyright." Even at first blush a sharp contrast with the primary definition is evident. The analogic comparison retains only a very limited sense of the original term, as is common in most analogies. But we may still gain a stronger sense of the analogy's operation by devoting attention to what elements of the definition serve as the core of the comparison. In this usage of piracy, the notion of statelessness has been lost, as has the strong implication of force or violence. What remains is the idea of taking without permission. But this definition also makes explicit a concept that was only implicit in the primary definition—the idea that the taking is "for one's own profit."

The mechanism by which these figurative pirates profit is made clear by the historical examples of this usage offered by the *OED*. The first example, and thus one of the very earliest if not *the* earliest uses of the term in print in English, is drawn from Philip Luckombe's 1771 edition of *The History and Art of Printing* and reads, "They . . . would suffer by this act of piracy, since it was likely to prove a very bad edition." Luckombe is describing the then common practice of "literary piracy," in which unscrupulous printers took advantage of the functional limits of copyright enforcement and produced unauthorized editions of popular books for sale at a considerable discount, relative to the authorized edition. A later example, drawn from Sir David Brewster's 1855 biography, *Memoirs of Newton,* refers to Isaac Newton's efforts to protect his invention of the reflecting telescope from "foreign piracy." In each of these examples, the mechanism by which the "pirates" profit is the production and distribution of substitute goods, whether goods subject to copyright, like books, or goods subject to patent, like telescopes and other mechanical inventions.

The use of piracy to describe these activities transpired despite the ready availability of the near synonym that Litman points toward in the above-cited passage: *counterfeiting.* While in a contemporary context, the term counterfeiting is almost exclusively associated with the illicit reproduction of currency, the term was for many years used to describe what the *OED* terms "fraudulent imitation" or "imitat[ion] [. . .] with intent to deceive." One of the earliest references in English to counterfeiting is drawn from Chaucer's *Canterbury Tales* and refers to personal letters being stolen and counterfeited. Thus, the term "counterfeit" has a long history of association with the literary arts, and its common usage for actions that might now be described as piracy is reflected in Richard Hakluyt's 1590 introduction to "The True Pictures and Fashions of the People in that Part of America Now Called Virginia, Discovured By Englishmen." Hakluyt closes with the following entreaty/warning:

> I heartily Request thee, that if any seek to Counterfeit this my book (for in this day many are so malicious that they seek to gain by other mens' labors) thou would give no credit unto such counterfeited Drawghte. For diverse secret marks lie hidden in my pictures, which will breed Confusion unless they be well observed. ("True Picture")

Hakluyt's stated approach to combatting "counterfeit editions" of his book is steganography—the embedding of hidden data within a product to facilitate verification or tracking—is currently being revisited in a digital context as a so-called "anti-piracy" measure. But it is worth noting that, for Hakluyt, there was a clear distinction between piracy and the kind of counterfeiting described here. Hakluyt's accounts of his attempts to discover the Northwest Passage are replete with accounts of the depredations of pirates. In a 1577 account, he notes the degree to which local populations in the New World had been terrorized by buccaneers:

> At our landing the people fled from their poor cottages with shrieks and alarms, to warn their neighbours of enemies, but by gentle persuasions we reclaimed them to their houses. It seemeth they are often frighted with pirates, or some other enemies, that move them to such sudden fear. ("*Voyages*")

The concept of literary piracy was not yet in vogue when Hakluyt crafted his introductory warning, but given his experience with the consequences of physical piracy, it is easy to sense how the term *counterfeiting* would have seemed more apt to him.

Given the consistency with which transgressions against what would come to be called "intellectual property" were described as counterfeiting for nearly four centuries, extending from Middle English to Modern English, we do well to ask how it was that the term came to be supplanted by piracy. One clue lies in the different resonances of the terms *pirate* and *counterfeiter*. While both are understood to be criminals, the pirate is active and violent, whereas the counterfeiter is stealthy and non-threatening. While both participate in activities that can have profoundly damaging consequences for their victims, the pirate threatens life and limb (there is good reason why the peg-leg and the hook are part of the stereotypical image of the pirate), while the counterfeiter threatens only economic harm. Both figures have been heavily romanticized. The pirate is romanticized for a putative roguish charm. This trope has played out in popular culture from at least Gilbert and Sullivan ("It is, it is a glorious thing to be a Pirate King!") through Errol Flynn, and continues into the present with Johnny Depp's portrayal of the charming reprobate Captain Jack Sparrow in the *Pirates of the Caribbean* movie series. The figure of the counterfeiter, by no means as commonplace in popular culture, is nevertheless romanticized for skill as an artisan (of a sort) and for stealth. But when push comes to shove, the pirate is by far the more threatening of the two figures (especially if a plank is involved) and for this reason it is, and has been, in publishers' interests to characterize infringers not as nonviolent, stealthy counterfeiters, but as violent, rapacious pirates.

The act of selling pirated editions of copyrighted works is widely understood as illegal and usually considered unethical. The most common argument in favor of piracy is that the copyright holders have not taken into account the realities of local economies and that their products would be wholly unavailable were it not for piracy. This justification is commonly applied to the pirating of computer software in developing countries. The U.S., by contrast, is thought to be so wealthy and so laden with purchasing opportunities that piracy of cultural property seems reflective of a particularly dogged criminality.

In a U.S. context, piracy serves two functions. The first is undercutting the prices for legitimate copies, and the second is delivering copies in a preferred media format before the availability of legitimate copies. The decision to purchase a pirated product is thus grounded in some combination of financial and chronological expediency. But opportunities for piracy in the U.S. are somewhat limited because if time is taken into account, virtually any cultural artifact can be had at an affordable price.

Consider the life cycle of a typical hardcover book. The first edition hardback is available at a premium (the printed list price) for those who wish to purchase it in the first week. Assuming the book is popular, it then reaches best-seller lists and is subject to discounts typically in the neighborhood of 20–30% at major booksellers. Over the course of a few months, used copies begin filtering into used bookstores and online sellers, including Amazon.com, which helpfully lists the availability of used books alongside the prices of new books. If a book's popularity warrants, it might also be available at an even more substantial discount through book clubs. For example, the Book-of-the Month Club offshoot Zooba is currently selling a selection of best-sellers for $9.95, shipping included. And many hardcovers are ultimately remaindered and moved to bargain bins in a last stab at generating a few dollars. Following on the heels of the hardcover there might be both a trade paperback (printed on fairly high quality paper) and a so-called "mass market" paperback (printed on newsprint-grade paper).

For Laura Hillebrand's immensely popular 2001 book, *Seabiscuit: An American Legend* initial list prices ranged from $25.95 for the brand-new hardcover to $7.99 for the mass-market paperback released two years later. Many used copies of the various editions are now available via Amazon, with prices typically starting at under a dollar. In the five years since Hillebrand's book was released, editions of varying quality have become available at virtually any price point. Because the U.S. book publishing market offers such a broad array of purchasing opportunities (and the reasonable certainty that its products can be purchased at very low cost within a few years) there is almost no piracy of books within the United States.

But in the case of compact discs and DVDs, there are not as many editions and not as many gradations in the ultimate prices. The 2003 film version of *Seabiscuit* is available in two DVD editions, fullscreen and widescreen. Both initially listed for $14.98, but used copies are now available for under $3 at Amazon.com. The compact disc of the soundtrack was initially listed for $18.98 (note that this price, for an ancillary product derived from the film, was initially $4 more than the film itself) and used copies are now for sale for roughly $5.

The book now commands only a tiny fraction of its original price (excluding first editions that might command a premium on the collector's market). The DVD of the film can be had for roughly a fifth of its original price. And the compact disc still commands over a quarter of its original list price. But all are ultimately affordable. It is somewhat surprising, given the steep decline in prices over the course of only two years, that many consumers still prefer to purchase pirated discs. Nevertheless, piracy persists in most major American cities, as an August, 2003 column by the late *Variety* columnist Army Archerd ably demonstrates:

> On a busy and blistering Sunday (the thermometer was topping 97) the famous "Alley" between Santee Street and Maple Avenue, in the heart of L.A.'s fashion district, was body-to-body with shoppers. Bargains are the byword here and $5 is the going rate for a DVD. I'd been tipped by a civilian friend, Sylvia Gordon, who'd told me she and Helen Kuhn bought "Seabiscuit" there last week. I thought it was impossible, but decided to see for myself. I located a young entrepreneur standing outside one of the hundreds of multi-merchandise stores. Yes, he had a DVD of "Seabiscuit." [NOTE: the film had opened July 25, roughly two weeks before Archerd visited the "Alley."] "Anything else?" I asked. He pulled out a black bag containing a fistful of DVDs, including "Pirates of the Caribbean: The Curse of the Black Pearl."

In the case of the pirated *Seabiscuit* DVD (and also the pirated *Pirates*) the counterfeit DVDs were taking advantage of the now-enforced pause between theatrical release and DVD release. These DVDs also preyed upon the disparity between movie theater ticket prices, which had crested at $10 in Los Angeles, and the possibility of several people watching the film in a home theater for $5.

Buyers knowingly assume a certain measure of risk when purchasing pirated copies. Many of the copies sold illegally on the street are poor quality transfers from videotape or, worse, videorecordings of film screenings shot from within a movie theater. Archerd exhibited an appropriate measure of skepticism as he trolled the "Alley":

> When I asked the Santee Street salesman about the quality of the DVDs, he assured me they were top quality—and produced a portable DVD player on the spot to allay any fears. My civilian friends who had told me of this illegal "treasure trove" were more trusting when they purchased "Seabiscuit": When they arrived home to play their bright and shiny new discs, they found them to be blanks. (Archerd)

But a substantial enough pool of buyers, unwilling to wait for legitimate copies to drop into their price range, or seduced by the relative inexpensiveness of the pirated DVDs, continues to drive this market.

A May, 2005 *New York Times* article states that the number of street vendors illegally selling goods of all kinds, from counterfeit handbags to pirated CDs and DVDs had "grown exponentially" in recent years. The *Times* article offers a reasonably clear picture of the shoppers who frequent street vendors. For some, there is an inherent appeal in participating in activities that defy the law. The article reports: "Some customers revel in the idea that some of the stuff is stolen, that it 'fell off the back of the truck.' That almost never happens. Virtually none of the items sold are authentic, but many tourists, young and old, don't seem to care" (Rozhon and Thorner).

In the U.S. "outlaw" activities have a demonstrable appeal. A variation of the same anti-authoritarian impulse that drives hackers, rockers, and rappers manifests itself in the grey markets of the American metropolis. The dynamic is redoubled by the fact that in an international context the U.S.'s adherence can fairly be described as both tardy and fitful. In the nineteenth century, the U.S had a well-earned reputation as a nation that embraced piracy. Charles Dickens famously toured the States decrying the pirated editions of his novels that effectively wiped out the market for legitimate editions. As a British author, Dickens was directly harmed by the U.S.'s refusal to honor international copyright laws. Dickens's campaigns for international copyright standards helped pave the way for the 1886 Berne Convention for the Protection of Literary and Artistic Works, initially signed by ten nations—Belgium, France, Germany, Haiti, Italy, Liberia, Spain, Switzerland, Tunisia, and the United Kingdom.

A century later, the U.S. was steadfastly refusing to sign the Berne Convention. One of the U.S.'s principal objections was that U.S. Copyright law provided for fixed copyright terms, whereas the Berne signatories had adopted a floating term based on the life of the author plus a number of additional years. Even after adopting its own "life plus" standard in the 1976 revision, the U.S. delayed signing Berne until 1989. Arguably, the U.S. should never have signed. In addition to the excessive duration of "life plus" standards (exemplified by the U.S.'s current "life of the author plus seventy years" base term for copyrights) the Berne Convention reflects its grounding in the moral rights tradition that the U.S. arguably rejected when, in the Constitution, copyrights and patents were cast as grants from the public to authors and inventors. The continuing popularity of street markets selling pirated goods suggests that U.S. citizens sometimes reflect their nation's historical status as reluctant latecomers to copyright as commonly practiced in an international context.

The *Times* article's reporters also asked the customers at the street markets whether they were at all concerned about the laws that might have been violated by the vendors, and by their own purchases. The responses suggest a calculated disregard for the potential consequences of piracy:

> Kaila's mother, Jacqueline Thompson, said she was somewhat bothered that the artists and musicians who made the CDs and DVDs were not getting their fair percentage, and the young tourists from Toronto said if they knew the vendors were selling illegally they would not be buying.
> But Ms. Wilson, the shopper from Chicago, said she didn't particularly care. "Whatever," she said, keeping her eye on the vendor, who was making change. "I'm not the one who's going to get into trouble." (Rozhon and Thorner)

Ms. Wilson is offering a realistic assessment of the law as it regards *physical* piracy. The purchasers of obviously counterfeit and pirated merchandise are never targeted in the occasional raids and sting operations directed at stemming the tide of unauthorized and illegal goods. To a certain extent, the poor quality of most of these goods functions as its own enforcement mechanism. The purchaser of the fake Louis Vuitton handbag with the handle that breaks after three days of use is out of luck, unless she can locate the vendor, and the vendor is usually a moving target.

Digital media have transformed the economics of street piracy. The purchaser of the blank DVD supposed to have housed *Seabiscuit* is just as out of luck as the purchaser of the fake handbag, but the costs of producing a high quality copy of the film have dropped so low that an increasing number of vendors are opting to sell DVDs that rival the quality of commercial releases. That said, most consumers could easily distinguish between the packaging of a legitimately released commercial DVD, and the packaging of a pirated DVD. By and large, consumers of pirated DVDs are knowingly purchasing an illicit product as a substitute for a legitimate purchase.

Few would argue that the content industries do not have a legitimate interest in stemming the traffic in pirated physical editions of their copyrighted works. While some of the more heavy-handed enforcement techniques trigger occasional outcries from participants in the peer-to-peer debates, there is general acknowledgment that the presence of a $5 DVD copy of *Pirates of the Caribbean* competes unfairly with the $10.50 tickets at the local cineplex. Nevertheless, the evident comfort many consumers demonstrate when shopping for obviously pirated goods stems from a baseline sense that piracy of copyrighted materials is, at least with respect to *their* particular purchases, a victimless crime. Any of a number of rationalizations will serve to explain away the purchase of a pirated DVD. Parents point to the high costs of babysitting. Experienced filmgoers point out, with some merit, that not every film is "worth" the cost of a full-price admission (thereby according to themselves the "right" to pay a lower price whenever possible). Smokers, and those who enjoy alcohol during films, point out that these products are forbidden in movie theaters. (My thanks to a student who will remain nameless who offered this last explanation for her dorm-based consumption of unauthorized copies of Hollywood films—as a non-smoker, this never would have occurred to me—and I suspect smoking bans do play a significant role in declining attendance at movie theaters). Whatever the rationalization, on a purchase-by-purchase basis, the harm caused by physical piracy seems minor, hardly even worthy of the piracy analogy. No cutlasses are swung. No one is sent plunging toward Davy Jones's locker. In the purchaser's mind, a movie studio that already has too much money has lost, at most, a few dollars.

Given the evident failure of the piracy analogy to prompt a qualitative shift in consumers' purchases of physical goods, one might have expected the content industries to develop a term with more precision or more rhetorical power to address the unauthorized downloading of copyrighted materials. But from the content industries' perspective, any time a potential consumer takes unauthorized possession of a physical *or digital* copy of a protected work, a crime has been committed. The association of these crimes with physical violence and rapaciousness is, from the content industries' perspective, entirely appropriate, whether the copyrighted work in question is physical or digital.

The content industry's strategy of extending the piracy analogy throughout virtual spaces has a long history. Napster was routinely described by the RIAA as a facilitator of piracy, and this usage was generally adopted by the mainstream media. With this baseline established, the RIAA settled on a second target: my.mp3.com.

In early 2000 one of the RIAA's member corporations (UMG Recordings) sued the Internet start-up mp3.com for having inaugurated a service called my.mp3.com. The service was an offshoot of the popular mp3.com, which in its heyday housed sixteen listening years' worth of audio content from performers ranging from rank amateurs to recognized acts like David Bowie and Linkin Park. The my.mp3 service was grounded in recognition that many users of peer-to-peer services simply wished to have access, in digital form, to music they had already purchased. My.mp3 asked users to verify their purchase of a compact disc by inserting the disc into their computer. Once my.mp3 verified physical possession of the disc, it allowed that user, employing a proprietary software protocol called "Beam-It" to access the contents of that disc via the Internet from any computer. The My.mp3 service was especially popular with Internet users who did not wish to transport their compact discs to and from their workplaces. With the "Beam-It" software, users could quickly verify their ownership (or, at the very least, *possession*) of a number of compact discs, and then quickly access their favorite music from office computers, or *any* computer connected to the Internet.

mp3.com purchased physical copies (at retail prices) of all of the music it made available to its users. And my.mp3 required users of the Beam-It software to stipulate that they were, in fact, loading copies of legally acquired discs into their computers. mp3.com CEO Michael Robertson clearly believed his company was on the right side of copyright law, as the following excerpt from a March, 2000 *Wired* article indicates. Robertson argues,

> The whole purpose of copyright law is to guarantee access to copyrighted materials for consumers. The copyright law is not to protect copyright holders, it is to guarantee access for consumers to create a viable marketplace, and that's exactly what we are doing. (qtd. in King)

Robertson's statement is, no doubt, grounded in a reasonably standard interpretation of the "Progress" clause in the U.S. Constitution that served as basis for the first U.S. copyright law. In this understanding, the central forms of intellectual property protection (i.e., copyrights and patents) are offered by the people, via Congress, and *for the people,* as an incentive for further production from authors and inventors. This represents a subtle but significant break from a broader European tradition in which the so-called "natural rights" of the author or inventor function as the bases for intellectual property protections. The 1991 Supreme Court's ringing endorsement of copyright's inherent public bias in the *Feist* case (once again: "The primary objective of copyright is not to reward the labor of authors, but '[t]o promote the Progress of Science and useful Arts.'") almost certainly emboldened Robertson as he set about developing the my.mp3.com service.

Robertson even agreed with the RIAA that Napster was enabling piracy. As the Napster case was still wending its way through the courts, Robertson was sharply critical of his fellow RIAA defendant.

> There have been a lot of comparisons of my.mp3.com and Napster, and nothing could be further from the truth. Napster is built entirely on pirated music. We are helping grow the music industry by encouraging people to buy more products.
>
> [. . .]
>
> When you talk about piracy you are talking about taking music without paying for it. The focus for the industry has been on how to stop people from taking that music. That's the wrong focus. The right focus is how do you make it easier for them to pay. You give

> them all those different price points, like the movie industry does. If you are properly filling all the channels with price points, you de-emphasize the need for piracy. (qtd. in King)

Robertson distinguished my.mp3.com from Napster because, unlike Napster, my.mp3.com did not allow users to *download* music files. The "Beam-It" software streamed music, essentially functioning as a personal jukebox for each user. Robertson grounds his definition of piracy in the phenomenon at the heart of *physical* piracy of cultural artifacts: unauthorized duplication. By contrast, the "Beam-It" software was designed to prevent users from accessing music that they had not purchased or possessed. my.mp3.com could reasonably describe its the vast majority of its interactions with its users as a coordinated, cooperative exchange between two legitimate owners of the music in question.

When, in January 2001, a group of RIAA affiliates led by UMG Recordings filed suit against mp3.com, they asked the court to award statutory damages of $150,000 per work infringed. Because mp3.com had invested a significant chunk of its successful initial public offering of stock into purchasing physical copies of compact discs, its library of works available for transmission to "Beam-It" users was 45,000 discs deep. A full judgment against my.mp3.com would have prompted damages of over sixty *billion* dollars.

mp3.com countersued, and in the countersuit, Robertson continued to insist that my.mp3.com's service was well removed from both "theft" and "piracy." The complaint reads, in part:

> RIAA and Rosen, on behalf of and in concert with the RIAA's recording industry members, have waged a campaign to impugn and disparage mp3.com as supporting music 'theft,' 'piracy' and other disreputable practices, and to use these false allegations to disrupt and interfere with mp3.com's financial and business relationships. (Boehlert)

At the time of the countersuit, Robertson was also embroiled in a feisty exchange of open letters with RIAA President Hilary Rosen. While the exchanges grew increasingly testy, Robertson seemed to maintain a sense of humor about the unfolding events: "Hilary still has my cell phone number[. . .] . It's not personal. It's business. But when somebody sues you for $60 billion, it's tough to stay friends." (Boehlert)

It is likely that Rosen's February 8 open letter eradicated any traces of friendship between Robertson and Rosen. While the RIAA had, to that point, exercised some care and restraint in its descriptions of my.mp3.com and its services, the gloves came off, and Robertson was saddled with the charge he had so scrupulously worked to avoid. Rosen wrote:

> The claims in the lawsuit are ridiculous. This is a transparent attempt on the part of mp3.com to silence criticism of its infringing tactics. It won't work. Our record is clear in distinguishing legitimate uses of MP3 technology from piracy. The lawsuit against mp3.com has nothing to do with MP3 technology. It has to do with mp3.com, the company, taking music they don't own and haven't licensed to offer new services to make money for themselves. And there is nothing illegal in my saying so. (Rosen)

While Rosen's statements may not have been illegal, they *were* unethical. The term *piracy* does not appear in the complaint filed with the court in the mp3.com case, and with good reason. The only references to piracy in Title 17 of the U.S. Code, which houses copyright law, are to the "Piracy and Counterfeiting Amendments Act of 1982." As the date suggests, this act was directed at the piracy of *physical* copies of various media, especially sound recordings and motion pictures. Even so, the RIAA was not shy about bandying the charge of piracy when it believed the facts—however marginally—supported the charge. The RIAA-affiliated corporations who sued Napster made piracy the centerpiece of their arguments, with variants of the term appearing dozens of times in the Napster complaint. A single exemplary sentence adequately conveys the tone: "Napster has [. . .] misused and is misusing the remarkable potential of the Internet, essentially running an online bazaar devoted to the pirating of music." With the Napster case serving as a baseline, it becomes clear that the absence of references to piracy in the my.mp3.com case was *not* accidental. The RIAA did not invoke the term because it understood that my.mp3.com *did not facilitate piracy*.

The worst that could fairly be said of my.mp3.com was what U.S. District Judge Jed Rakoff wrote in his grant of partial summary judgment: "defendant is re-playing for the subscribers converted versions of the recordings it copied, without authorization, from plaintiffs' copyrighted CDs" (*UMG Recordings*). While this judge went on to describe this re-playing as "a presumptive case of infringement under the Copyright Act" he did not equate my.mp3.com with piracy. Rakoff's final ruling, in which he awards the RIAA affiliates damages in the amount of $118,000,000, contains a passage in which he acknowledges that Robertson's actions to avoid facilitating piracy were a mitigating factor that limited the amount of damages (though the damages were nonetheless substantial enough to shutter mp3.com). Rakoff writes:

> I also credit that portion of Mr. Robertson's testimony in which he indicated that, even from the outset, he shunned the kind of lawless piracy seemingly characteristic of some others operating in this area. While the defendant's willful copyright infringement was a very serious transgression, defendant's otherwise responsible conduct is an appropriate mitigating factor for the Court to take into account. (Ruling in mp3.com)

Had Robertson been able to afford an appeal, my.mp3.com might well have won, as Judge Rakoff's decision was grounded in an interpretation of copyright law that deserved to be challenged. In a critical passage, Rakoff argues: "Copyright [. . .] is not designed to afford consumer protection or convenience but, rather, to protect the copyright holders' property interests." On its face, it is difficult to reconcile this interpretation of copyright with Justice O'Connor's clear emphasis on the public interest in the *Feist* decision.

By placing the copyright holders' property interest ahead of the public's reasonable desire to access information it had *already* purchased, Rakoff not only wrongly decided the my.mp3.com case, he turned away from two centuries of precedents and legal interpretations that had reinforced the public's access to and reasonable use of information. At the time of the my.mp3.com case, Jessica Litman recalls participating in an electronic mailing list with other law professors, and she reports that "the majority of professors on that list insisted that the fair use privilege shielded the copying that Robertson got sued for"

("War and Peace"). But Judge Rakoff conducted his own fair use analysis, and arrived at the opposite result. That's where the case ends.

Litman argues further that despite the RIAA's eventual victory, the lawsuit against my.mp3.com was strategically unwise:

> Now, again, I can see why people were angry, but they could have reached a settlement calling for modest royalties that would have exceeded anything that's being collected today under section 112 for ephemeral copies. Choosing to litigate the entire site out of business sent precisely the wrong message to other innovators. If you're going to get buried with a stake through your heart even if you purchase a license for what you are doing, and try to obey what your lawyers reasonably conclude the law says, why even try? ("War and Peace")

This stifling of innovation, the very *opposite* of the promotion of science and useful arts, is the inevitable consequence of a debate that has been notable for its rhetorical excesses and inaccuracies.

When Hilary Rosen publicly charged Michael Robertson's company with piracy, she knew that my.mp3.com was not adding to the number of unauthorized MP3 files circulating on the Internet. But she and her colleagues in the RIAA publicly pretended to observe no significant distinctions between my.mp3.com and Napster. In a contemporaneous article, an unnamed music industry executive succinctly summarized the music industry's stance, claiming: "mp3.com is Napster in sheep's clothing." (qtd. in Macavinta)

Lawrence Lessig has properly described the content industries' attempted *re*definition of piracy as having "at its core an extraordinary idea that is almost certainly wrong." In *Free Culture* Lessig outlines the arguments put forward by the RIAA, MPAA, and their cohorts as follows:

> Creative work has value; whenever I use, or take, or build upon the creative work of others, I am taking from them something of value. Whenever I take something of value from someone else, I should have their permission. The taking of something of value

> from someone else without permission is wrong. It is
> a form of piracy. (18)

Indeed, each incremental step of this distilled argument is almost certainly wrong. It is possible to use, take, or build on others' creative work without in any way diminishing the value of their work. Indeed, as Rebecca Moore Howard has argued, contemporary scholarship absolutely depends on building upon others' work. There are many circumstances when a requirement to secure permission would be recognized as unnecessary, or would result in *de facto* censorship. Appropriation without permission is central to the practices of journalism, scholarship, and criticism, to say nothing of the myriad artistic statements that draw upon and repurpose earlier works. Characterizing this range of cultural practices as not merely theft, but as piracy, radically overstates the content industries' case. Lessig encapsulates this argument as "if there is a value, then someone must have a right to that value" and suggests that this approach is, in addition to the above-cited flaws, singularly un-American. Lessig writes: "in our tradition, intellectual property is an instrument. It sets the groundwork for a richly creative society but remains subservient to the value of creativity" (*Free Culture* 33) Or rather, it *should*. Or perhaps it once *did* remain subservient to creativity, but it doesn't anymore. The successful public branding of Michael Robertson as a "pirate," raises a serious question as to just how much creativity and innovation will be lost because the U.S. is, apparently, incapable of conducting the debate over peer-to-peer technologies with simultaneous attention to nuance, civility, and basic fairness.

True to his prescient form, Richard Stallman was among the first to identify and decry the content industries' campaign to broaden the meaning of piracy. In his 1996 catalog of "21 Words to Avoid" (since expanded and more accurately retitled "Some Confusing or Loaded Words and Phrases That Are Worth Avoiding") Stallman offers this clear, direct, and concise critique of a rhetorical shift that he lays at the doorstep of the content industries:

> Publishers often refer to prohibited copying as "piracy." In this way, they imply that illegal copying is ethically equivalent to attacking ships on the high seas, kidnapping and murdering the people on them.

> If you don't believe that illegal copying is just like kidnapping and murder, you might prefer not to use the word "piracy" to describe it. Neutral terms such as "prohibited copying" or "unauthorized copying" are available for use instead. Some of us might even prefer to use a positive term such as "sharing information with your neighbor." (191)

Unfortunately, as the next chapter details, Stallman's proposed positive term, "sharing." is now yet another contested site in the increasingly corrosive debate over the future of ideas in digital contexts.

5 The Problem of "Sharing" in Digital Environments

The rhetorical positioning of peer-to-peer exchanges as "sharing" fails to acknowledge the special nature of digital media. Prior to the advent of digital technologies, sharing a particular resource necessarily implied at least momentary depletion of that resource. The person offering the resource would lose at least the use of the resource for the time that the resource was being shared. In *The Future of Ideas,* Lawrence Lessig helpfully casts this distinction as one between "rivalrous" and "non-rivalrous" resources, and observes:

> The system of control that we erect for rivalrous resources (land, cars, computers) *is not necessarily appropriate* for nonrivalrous resources (ideas, music, expression). Indeed, the *same system for both kinds of resources may do real harm.* Thus, a legal system, or a society generally, must be careful to tailor the kind of control to the kind of resource. One size won't fit all. (96)

The colloquial understand of "sharing" is wholly rooted in the division or apportioning of rivalrous resources. Lessig's examples effectively spotlight the dramatic difference between sharing rivalrous and nonrivalrous resources. If I agree to share my car or my laptop with someone, I understand that there will be times that I will not have access to those resources. But if I share an idea, we both have the idea. And if I "share" an MP3 file by serving it to others via a peer-to-peer network, my resource is *never* depleted. Indeed, very nearly the opposite is true, as its presence on the network facilitates the creation of additional copies of that file.

The old proverb states, you can not eat your cake and have it too. But the ready reproducibility of digital media means that, as a practical matter, one can offer the use of a resource without any loss of access or availability. In a peer-to-peer context you can eat your cake, allow others to eat it, and still have just as much cake as you started out with (and perhaps more).

The band Cake formed in Sacramento in 1991, and, as is the case with most popular bands, many of its songs are readily available for unauthorized downloads via peer-to-peer networks. Cake is not an especially prolific band. Since 1994, the band has released a total of five full-length CDs. In August of 2005, the Limewire peer-to-peer program, using the GNUtella protocol, offered pointers to over 200 Cake songs, more than double the number of songs officially released by the band. By contrast, the fully licensed iTunes Music Store housed 95 songs by the band—the whole of the bands' officially released output. Limewire is thus a space where fans of Cake can find not only the bulk of the band's officially released recordings, but also recordings of live performances, demos, and rarities that, for whatever reason, did not receive an official release. On Limewire, fans of the band not only have their Cake, they "share" it, too.

Purchasing Cake's official oeuvre from iTunes would cost roughly $95, exclusive of the costs associated with broadband connectivity to the Internet. The cost of all of that Cake plus all of the ephemera available on Limewire is, at first blush, nil. But there are costs that must be borne by those who distribute copyrighted material via networks like the GNUtella network at the heart of Limewire. The most dramatic costs are those associated with the lawsuits that have been filed by the RIAA with some regularity since September 2003. Because hardcore fans of musicians can reasonably be expected to comb the Internet for any scrap of music by their favorite performers, many musicians were open in expressing their discomfort with the RIAA's lawsuits. A September 2003 article in the *New York Times* featured this particularly sharp comment: "'On one hand, the whole thing [the RIAA lawsuit campaign] is pretty sick,' said John McCrea, a singer and songwriter in the rock band Cake. 'On the other hand, I think it'll probably work.'" (qtd. in Strauss)

McCrea's implicit concern for fans caught up in the lawsuit campaign was counterbalanced by other musicians like Loudon Wainwright III, who is quoted in the same *Times* article as supporting the

The Problem of "Sharing" in Digital Environments

Quality	#	Name	Type	Size	Speed
★★★★★	44	Cake -- Never There	mp3	2,475 KB	T1
★★★★★	28	Cake - Short Skirt, Long Jacket	mp3	3,252 KB	T1
★★★★★	26	Cake -- No Phone	mp3	5,428 KB	Cable/DSL
★★★★★	25	cake - perhaps, perhaps, perhaps	mp3	2,250 KB	T1
★★★★★	19	Rock And Roll Lifestyle	mp3	3,445 KB	T1
★★★★★	13	Daria	mp3	3,501 KB	T1
★★★★★	13	Cake - Let Me Go	mp3	3,257 KB	Cable/DSL
★★★★★	12	Cake - I Will Survive	mp3	4,855 KB	T1
★★★★★	12	Cake - Sheep Go To Heaven	mp3	4,440 KB	T1
★★★★★	12	Cake - pretty pink ribbon	mp3	4,417 KB	Cable/DSL
★★★★★	12	Creep (Radiohead cover)	mp3	3,665 KB	Cable/DSL
★★★★★	3	Cake - The Distance	mp3	2,822 KB	T1
★★★★★	3	Cake - Love You Madly	mp3	3,719 KB	Cable/DSL
★★★★★	2	096 - Cake - I Will Survive	mp3	4,864 KB	Cable/DSL
★★★★★	2	097 - Cake -- Never There	mp3	2,574 KB	Cable/DSL
★★★★★	2	Cake -- No Phone	mp3	5,428 KB	Cable/DSL
★★★★★	2	Cake -- Stick Shifts and Safety Belts	mp3	2,004 KB	T3 or Higher
★★★★★	2	098 - cake - Short Skirt Long Jacket	mp3	4,868 KB	Cable/DSL
★★★★★	2	cake - friend is a four letter word	mp3	3,154 KB	Cable/DSL
★★★★		Cake - Frank Sinatra	mp3	3,753 KB	Cable/DSL
★★★★		TV - Smallville Soundtrack -- Cake - Love You Madly	mp3	3,719 KB	Cable/DSL
★★★★		Wheels	mp3	4,589 KB	Cable/DSL
★★★★		Cake - Perhaps, Perhaps, Pe	mp3	2,250 KB	Modem
★★★★		Cake - He's Going the Distance	mp3	2,822 KB	Cable/DSL
★★★★		09 Love You Madly	mp3	3,719 KB	Cable/DSL

Figure 6. Cake songs available via the Limewire peer-to-peer client.

lawsuits: "If you're going to break the law, the hammer is going to come down." Wainwright had also written a song entitled "Something for Nothing" that acidly surveys the peer-to-peer phenomenon. On one recorded version of this song, Wainwright spits out the final chorus:

> You can pull one of my songs right out of thin air.
> Bootleg and download me, see if I care. In love, war
> and cyberspace, everything's fair. And it's okay to
> steal 'cause it's so nice to share.

Ironically, "Something for Nothing" is known to many listeners in a version broadcast on British disk jockey John Peel's radio program long before it was ever officially released. For over a year, the song was the subject of some discussion but commercially unavailable. Then, roughly six months before the song's initial official release (albeit in a different and arguably inferior version) on Wainwright's 2003 live album, "So Damn Happy," one website took Wainwright at his word and posted a bootleg MP3 of Wainwright's performance, where it remained available in 2006.

The RIAA's own press release on the day it inaugurated its lawsuit campaign acknowledges that one of the purposes was a kind of "education" for the general public. Alligator Records President Bruce Iglauer is quoted as follows:

> If this proliferation of the theft of the creations of artists continues, less and less music will be recorded. The public must be educated about the real results stealing [sic] music from its creators.
>
> It is unfortunate that the problem of illegal 'sharing' of copyrighted music has grown to the point where legal action is necessary, but that is the case. Until such time as the public is jarred into awareness, it is the sad necessity that the people who create and own the music must aggressively defend themselves from having their creations stolen. (RIAA, "Recording Industry to Begin Collecting Evidence")

The "lack of awareness" Iglauer points up here was by no means limited to an apparent failure to understand the potential economic harm peer-to-peer transfers might inflict on recording artists. Many users of peer-to-peer technologies simply did not believe that their activities would or could ever prompt any sort of legal entanglement. Litman has argued that because copyright law is "complicated, arcane, and counterintuitive [. . .] people don't believe the copyright law says what it does say." Litman further observes: "People do seem to buy into copyright norms, but they don't translate those norms into the rules that the copyright statute does; they find it very hard to believe that there's really a law out there that says the stuff that the copyright law says" (*Digital* 112). And even when users of peer-to-peer software did have a reasonable understanding of copyright law, many did not understand the basic operation of the software they were using, and were surprised to learn that they were distributing as well as downloading files.

The RIAA's lawsuits are often described as a campaign against "illegal downloading." This description is inaccurate. Even if we leave aside the sometimes complex question of whether a particular download is illegal, *de minimis,* fair use, or legal, the overarching fact is that to this point the RIAA has *never* sued an individual for downloading music off of the Internet. Rather, the RIAA has filed lawsuits against *uploaders* of music, and further, the lawsuits have typically targeted only those who are distributing in excess of 1,000 music files via the Internet.

There are a number of plausible strategic reasons for the RIAA's choice of targets in its lawsuit campaign, but one possible reason stands out. Were the RIAA to sue individuals who downloaded files without ever uploading them, the RIAA might well lose. The House reports leading to the 1991 Audio Home Recording Act make it clear that, at least at that time, home recording for private, non-commercial use was regarded as, if not wholly legal, certainly a *de minimis* violation of copyright. The legislative history for the AHRA is definitive on this point: "In short, the reported legislation would clearly establish that consumers cannot be sued for making analog or digital audio copies for private noncommercial use." We can infer that because of the Audio Home Recording Act's strong bias against prosecution of home users for making copies of media, the RIAA has wisely refrained from directly raising the legal question of whether personal and private copies merit the stiff penalties associated with copyright infringements. The act of uploading, by contrast, presents a more clear-cut case of copyright violation, as the uploader has, arguably, impinged on the distribution rights that are fundamental to copyright law.

The RIAA has consistently blurred the distinction in its own description of the campaign, tending to balance accurate references to the nature of its lawsuits with questionable references to "illegal downloading." The September 2003 press release announcing the inauguration of the lawsuit campaign provides a fine example of this strategy in operation:

> The Recording Industry Association of America (RIAA) announced today that its member companies have filed the first wave of what could ultimately be thousands of civil lawsuits against major offenders who have been illegally distributing substantial

> amounts (averaging more than 1,000 copyrighted music files each) of copyrighted music on peer- to-peer networks. The RIAA emphasized that these lawsuits have come only after a multi-year effort to educate the public about the illegality of unauthorized downloading. (RIAA, "Recording Industry to Begin Collecting Evidence")

This presentation features a subtle shift from an accurate statement (that the RIAA is targeting "offenders who have been illegally distributing substantial amounts" of copyrighted material) to an implied suggestion that downloading itself is illegal. The blending of terms has since become habitual for the RIAA. An April 2005 press release references "illegal downloading" and "illegal file sharers" before arriving at the more accurate characterization of the lawsuits as directed at individuals who allegedly "illegally distributed copyrighted music on the Internet":

> As part of its ongoing effort to protect the work of record labels, musicians, writers, producers and others from theft through illegal downloading, the Recording Industry Association of America (RIAA), on behalf of the major record companies, today announced a new wave of copyright infringement lawsuits against 725 illegal file sharers.
> The "John Doe" suits filed today cite the individuals for illegally distributing copyrighted music on the Internet via unauthorized peer-to-peer services such as Kazaa, eDonkey and Grokster. (RIAA "725 Additional")

The RIAA's consistent conflation of lawsuits against uploaders with the necessarily inaccurate blanket characterization of downloads as "illegal" has persuaded not only members of the general public but also journalists to present the peer-to-peer debates as, in effect, a pointless discussion about a settled question. If, as the RIAA suggests, downloads of music files are illegal, the only legitimate questions would be how and whether the law should be enforced.

But it is quite possible that certain Federal courts would rule that private and personal use of downloaded material is either legal, or a *de minimis* violation of copyright. Indeed, one of the U.S.'s closest neighbors has pursued just such an approach. Canadian copyright law is strikingly clear on the status of P2P downloads for personal use. *They are legal.* This relatively flat statement of the law is possible, in part, because Canadian copyright policies have focused on minimizing opportunities for conflict between consumers and owners of copyrighted material. Canada has adopted levies on most recordable media (examples include cassette tapes, CD-ROMs, and, for a time, MP3 players like the iPod) designed to compensate copyright holders for the multiple copies music fans could be expected to make. Canada's clarity on this point does not, however, extend to the status of uploading. And, as in the United States, the Canadian Recording Industry Association (CRIA) pursued a lawsuit campaign demanding that five major ISPs turn over the names of 29 uploaders of music files. But CRIA's campaign stalled in May 2005 when a Canadian appeals court ruled that CRIA had not provided enough solid evidence of infringement to warrant the invasion of privacy attendant in the release of users' names.

It is important to note that whether *uploading* constitutes infringement has yet to be fully tested in U.S. courts. To date, the vast majority of the lawsuits filed by the RIAA against uploaders of copyrighted materials have prompted settlements rather than court cases, and this means there are few precedents to draw upon. One notable exception is the case of *BMG Music et al. v. Gonzalez,* decided in the U.S. District Court for the Northern District of Illinois in early 2005. Both sides acknowledge that Gonzalez used Kazaa to download a substantial number of music files. Gonzalez's defense hinged, in part, on her claim that she did what she could to avoid redistributing these files. Gonzalez testified that when she became aware of the option to adjust Kazaa's settings, shortly after she began using the software, she changed the settings to foreclose further "sharing." While the initial complaint specified that Gonzalez had roughly 2,500 downloaded (and thus, potentially infringing) songs on her computer, the complaint was ultimately limited to 30 songs. Part of the trial process involved a lengthy review of Gonzalez' purchases, and it was established that many of the songs Gonzalez downloaded were in fact songs she had already purchased on compact discs.

According to the *Chicago Reader:*

> She wanted to be able to listen to them in any order, but didn't want to manually copy her whole CD collection onto her hard drive—she and her husband own about 250. She also used Kazaa to download a few songs she didn't own, but only to "listen to them and determine if they were something she would be interested in purchasing." (Mehr)

The thirty songs at the heart of the Gonzalez case were thus songs for which Gonzalez could offer no corresponding purchased CDs. The Court was dismissive of Gonzalez's claims to have been an "innocent infringer" and ruled against her, levying the statutory minimum penalty for willful infringement: $750 per song, or $22,500.

The Gonzalez case, the first of the RIAA lawsuits to go to trial, suggests that record companies are exercising some care to avoid directly raising the question of whether private home use of files is legal or not. While *all* of Gonzalez's music files would be described by the RIAA as "illegal downloads," the revision of the original complaint constitutes a tacit acknowledgment that the RIAA prefers for these cases to turn on *distribution*. In short, the RIAA took steps to ensure that the Gonzalez case focused on the allegedly brief period when Gonzalez's Kazaa settings allowed "sharing." The RIAA's consistent assertion has been that any time period, however brief, in which the software permits sharing opens the door to massive distribution and likely infringement.

> The RIAA's senior vice president for legal affairs, Stanley Pierre-Louis, acknowledges that Gonzalez may have been sharing her files only briefly and perhaps unwittingly, but he maintains that it doesn't matter. "The answer we have is if you'd turned the [share] default off we wouldn't have found you," he says. "That's the bottom line." (Mehr)

The problem is, as Pierre-Louis here acknowledges, "sharing" *is* the default setting for most peer-to-peer programs. Indeed, the richness of any peer-to-peer network depends upon many (if not most) users distributing at least some files. And Napster's most popular successor, Kazaa, has deployed questionable technical and rhetorical strategies in order to assure that users, knowingly or unknowingly, feed files to the Kazaa network.

The linchpin of the Kazaa peer-to-peer system is the so-called "shared folder." If a Kazaa user does not adjust the default settings for the program, this folder houses *all* of the songs that user has downloaded, and serves copies of all of those songs back out to the large network of individuals also using Kazaa. While the RIAA has responded with increasing derision to pleas of ignorance from peer-to-peer users ensnared in the RIAA lawsuit dragnet, it is clear that at least some generally ethical people were lulled into a false sense of security by the language on Kazaa's website.

Another Kazaa user caught up in the first wave of RIAA lawsuits was Lorraine Sullivan, who in September 2003 offered a statement to Congress that illustrates a degree of technical ignorance that was common among early users of Kazaa. Sullivan states:

> I mistakenly imagined that since Kazaa was still up and running while Napster had been forced to close down that the downloading I was personally responsible for was okay. I certainly never saw any sort of disclaimer on the original Kazaa website. I compared it to recording songs from the radio. I never willingly shared files with other users. I was not even fully aware of all the songs in "my" Kazaa file until I looked at it after receiving the Time Warner subpoena letter. As far as I was concerned the music I downloaded was for home, personal use. I made a play list of favorites and listened to it when I cleaned house or did homework. Part of the reason I downloaded songs I already owned on CD was because I didn't want to mix them manually and found it more convenient to have on my computer. I don't know how to "upload" songs on the computer either. I in no way financially benefited from nor intended to make a profit from the music I listened to. As far as I was concerned copyright infringement was what the people in Chinatown hawking bootlegged and fake CDs on the street corner were doing.

Sullivan's statement, while presented with a veneer of naiveté, actually presents a series of arguable defenses to the charge of copyright infringement. The first is that Kazaa had an obligation to warn her of the possible illegality of downloading copyrighted materials. Sullivan could not accurately state that no such warning exists on the Kazaa site, as Kazaa has included such warnings on its site since its inception. But the nature of the warnings is such that Sullivan could reasonably plead confusion. Consider this language from the first iteration of the Kazaa website, posted in October 2000:

> Something you have to keep in mind . . .
>
> Please do not infringe on the copyright of other people! Later this year we will introduce a payment system, with which you will be able to download copyrighted files at a very low cost. You will be able to enjoy the works of mainstream artists with a clean conscience and your favourite artist receives their well-earned royalties.
>
> Napster and Scour, two first-generation file-sharing services have both been sued and may be forced to shut down.
>
> Our mission is to create a community with a much broader scope than these services, a community where you can still enjoy the works of established artists, but with a clear conscience and at a very fair price! So—please be sensitive to the legal issues—do not share material that is copyrighted, such as MP3 files copied from your CDs. Support Kazaa for the next couple of months if you want to be able to enjoy the works of commercial artists on Kazaa with a clear conscience.

Amid a wealth of language suggesting that Kazaa was actively pursuing a resolution to its dicey status with respect to U.S. Copyright law, the company provides a wholly inadequate account of how infringement might occur, offering as its sole illustrative example of questionable usage, "MP3 files copied from your CDs." It is quite possible that Lorraine Sullivan could honestly state that she never copied music from her CDs into her computer. Indeed, her testimony suggests that she valued Kazaa precisely because it spared her the chore of loading CDs into her computer. It is likely that Sullivan's computer housed no MP3 files burned from her personal CD collection. Nevertheless, the Kazaa software's default settings ensured that she was amassing and effectively uploading a large compilation of MP3 files, and every time she booted up her computer, everything she had ever downloaded was served back up to Kazaa's network.

Sullivan also suggested that she had been wrongfully targeted in part because her fiancé had downloaded the software and in part because she allowed others to use her computer. These claims surely do not absolve her of her responsibility to develop a measure of awareness about the software on her personal computer. But because Sullivan claimed that her fiancé downloaded the software in August of 2001, Sullivan can point to the misleading language that was featured on the Kazaa website at the time:

> Kazaa in a Nutshell
>
> Kazaa is a media community, where millions community members can share their media files—audio, video, images and documents—with each other.

Without directly asserting that the service is legal, this language tacitly implies that this is the case by asserting that in the Kazaa "community [. . .] users can share." The site also featured "Terms of Service" that featured specific language warning against copyright infringement, but this language was positioned deep within the website so as to make it easily avoidable, leaving Kazaa's users with at least plausible deniability, and in many cases real ignorance of the site's warnings against potentially infringing uses of the software. It was indeed possible, as Sullivan testifies, "to never see any sort of disclaimer." But, as the old saw states, ignorance of the law is no excuse. Yet in her subsequent arguments, Sullivan presents a much stronger case for her use of Kazaa.

Sullivan next states that she compared her downloading of songs to the arguably legal action of recording songs off of the radio. Knowingly or not, Sullivan is articulating the principle at the heart of the Audio Home Recording Act " that consumers cannot be sued for making analog or digital audio copies for private noncommercial use." If one accepts Sullivan's analogy, that her use of Kazaa was comparable to making recordings off the radio, then the language in the House reports strongly supports her claim that her use was reasonable and ought not have triggered a lawsuit.

Sullivan then claims that she was unaware that her downloading of songs for personal use also positioned her as an uploader of these same music files. It can be argued that the term "peer-to-peer" itself constitutes a tacit acknowledgment that downloaders must also be uploaders if the network is to remain robust (though it should be remembered that the "peers" referenced are *computers,* not individuals). Many users, like Sullivan, were startled to learn that all of the files they had downloaded were routinely maintained and recirculated via their so-called "shared folders." This surprise is in part attributable to the disingenuous presentation of Kazaa's mechanics on the company's website.

Kazaa's description of how the "shared folder" functions is a masterpiece of misdirection. Kazaa inaugurates a section of its user guidebook entitled "Sharing and the P2P Philosophy" with this questionable definition: "Sharing is making your content available to other peer-to-peer users." The key point of slippage in this definition is Kazaa's use of "your content," which in practice meant not only content created by Kazaa users, but also content purchased or even momentarily possessed by Kazaa users. It should also be noted that "making content available" is a description that repositions "sharing" from its common meaning as a negotiated activity between individuals in a specific location or context, and extends the concept to the largely anonymous and ephemeral machine-based connections facilitated by peer-to-peer networks. Napster could plausibly claim to be fostering "community" to the extent that the software's chat functionality allowed users to communicate with one another, and survey one another's collections of music. These aspects of Napster's software encouraged many users to bond over a shared love of an obscure band or genre. While similar features are available within Kazaa, the default settings for the software allow for no instant messaging and no browsing of a given user's files. Typically, Kazaa users' interactions are limited to the anonymous transfer of files. Here we see the real consequence of the sharp difference between rivalrous and nonrivalrous resources. Sharing of rivalrous resources is typically achieved through negotiation and communication. As Kazaa demonstrates, a nonrivalrous, readily reproducible resource like MP3 files can be distributed without anything more than the most rudimentary negotiation. Indeed in Kazaa the "negotiation" typically transpires between a file seeker and a machine surreptitiously distributing the desired file. By contrast, Napster at least preserved opportunities for negotiation and communication, and this was arguably the outgrowth of a sincere commitment to community building among the developers of Napster's software.

Despite the suppression of community sustaining features in the Kazaa software, Kazaa's website repeatedly presented the software as facilitating collaborative relationships among the software's users. One egregious example of this rhetorical stratagem does considerable violence to Descartes:

> At Sharman Networks we have a saying:
> "I share, therefore we are."
> Responsible sharing is the cornerstone of a useful peer-to-peer experience. In order for everyone to benefit from the collaboration, users need to share appropriate files. Successful peer-to-peer is a two way street.

And, in order for Kazaa to benefit significantly from this "collaboration," users need to share appropriate*d* files. Kazaa's business model depends on selling advertisements, most of which are delivered to users' computers as part of their initial download of the Kazaa software in the form of additional adware. (The pop-up ads within Kazaa Media Desktop are so frequent and bothersome that they have prompted a small cottage industry of shareware programs designed to eliminate or suppress the ads.) Kazaa depends on its software being downloaded frequently in order to drive advertising revenue. Its popularity is tied directly to the availability of copyrighted popular music via its software. Kazaa, is, in effect, selling billboards on every inch of the "two-way street," and failing to adequately warn its users about the "one-way sign" that the RIAA has posted at the other end of the street.

Users who relied on the language of the Kazaa "Guide" that was in place prior to the RIAA lawsuits can legitimately claim that they were relying on information that failed to fully and fairly explain both the operation of the Kazaa software and the risks attendant to using it. In a critical paragraph, Kazaa manages to suggest that the default software setting that opened Cecilia Gonzalez to litigation is actually the "safest" option. I will quote the "Guide" at some length, and then illustrate how this section is structured to misdirect readers away from an informed understanding of the technology they are employing:

> The Kazaa Media Desktop peer-to-peer application is set up to allow the user to control what, and how much they share. You can:
>
> - Specify which files you share.
> - Decide how many files you allow to be downloaded by other KMD users at any one time (to minimize the impact on your computer and bandwidth capacity).
> - Decide whether to reply to instant messages from other users.
>
> When you select a folder to share, all files and subfolders inside that folder will be available for other KMD users to download. Please take great care not to accidentally share files that are illegal, confidential or which you do not have the right to distribute. You should not share your entire hard drive or My Documents folder.
>
> For this reason, it is safest to use 'My Shared Folder,' which will be set up automatically as the default folder. This means that all files inside 'My Shared Folder' are available for other KMD users to find and download from you. New files that you download will automatically go into 'My Shared Folder.'

Kazaa's statements regarding the levels of control available to users were all true. It *was* possible and not especially difficult to adjust the settings to achieve the goals outlined. But Kazaa's emphasis on the degree of control afforded to users was countered by the following paragraph's suggestion that the default settings are the "safest" option. For most any piece of information technology the default settings are, for many users, the *only* settings ever used. Anyone who doubts this need only begin tracking how many of their neighbors' and friends' VCRs are blinking "12:00." One of the unfortunate truths of the information age is that most people have become too impatient to read and understand the various user agreements and manuals that determine the limits for their use of technologies. And even if people *did* attempt to read this information, more often than not they would face skeins of impenetrable legalese that does not help them understand where the property lines are drawn. Kazaa's approach to peer-to-peer depended upon users' fatigue with technical and legal details. Indeed, Kazaa depended on many, if not most, users accepting the defaults.

From a legal standpoint, Kazaa's settings were and are potentially disastrous. Users who followed what was here described as the "safe" approach became distributors of every file they downloaded from Kazaa, and they continued serving files to Kazaa for however long their computers remained powered up and connected to the Internet. For many broadband users, this meant that they were constantly feeding files to the Kazaa network. These Kazaa users were "sharing" not because of any conscious commitment to exchange, but because the software's default settings imposed that on them.

The RIAA lawsuits have had one inarguably positive outcome: an increase in consumers' attentiveness to the user agreements and default settings of the peer-to-peer software that they are using. Increasingly, Kazaa users have taken control of their software and adjusted the default settings to protect themselves from RIAA lawsuits. In practical terms, this means that most Kazaa users now download songs without maintaining any songs in the "My Shared Folder." A small subset of Kazaa users, for whatever reason, choose to continue serving files to the network, while the majority of users are now "free riders." This pattern was also observed, years ago, on the Gnutella network. While the Kazaa front-end is user-friendly enough that it lured many users new to peer-to-peer, Gnutella clients have historically required a greater measure of technical knowledge. With most Gnutella clients, users exercise a higher level of control over their personal settings than with Kazaa. For this reason, the core conclusion of Eytan Adar and Bernardo Huberman's 2000 study of the usage patterns of Gnutella users—that roughly 70 percent of Gnutella users distribute no files—is perhaps not surprising. Thus, while peer-to-peer technologies are rooted in the establishment of level relationships among networked computers (the "peers" in peer-to-peer) the *people* using peer-to-peer technologies typically pursue imbalanced relationships. As a result, a small subset of peer-to-peer users account for the bulk of the distribution of authorized and unauthorized files to peer-to-peer networks, thereby assuming the bulk of the risks associated with the transmission of these files. It is these users who have earned the right to frame arguments that their activities constitute "sharing." By contrast, peer-to-peer users who scrupulously avoid making files available to others are not sharing, but *taking*.

The uncritical maintenance of "sharing" as an overarching metaphor for peer-to-peer file transfers distorts the debate. Thus, while advocates of peer-to-peer technologies are right to reject formulations that position them as thieves or pirates by dint of their participation on peer-to-peer networks, they also should acknowledge that peer-to-peer transfers are not a form of "sharing" as the term is conventionally understood. Yet the term "file sharing" has become so entrenched that it is used even by those who elsewhere demonstrate real sensitivity to the complexities of ownership and distribution in digital contexts.

For example, the Electronic Frontier Foundation is one of the finest and most important defenders of the public interest with respect to the Internet and digital media. I generally endorse the organization, often reference it in classroom discussions, and have cited its founders in my scholarly work. The front page of the EFF's website for many months featured a small ad that read: "Let the Music Play. Tired of being treated like a criminal for sharing music online?" The ad linked to a page headlined, "File-Sharing: It's Music to our Ears." While this pun is admittedly clever, the headline bespeaks an overly broad acceptance of "sharing" as a descriptor for the activities that drive peer-to-peer file transfers, especially when Kazaa's slippery usage of the term is taken into account.

The EFF has also maintained a Web page entitled "How Not to Get Sued by the RIAA for File-Sharing" that features the following advice:

> Make sure there are no potentially infringing files in your shared folder. This would ordinarily mean that your shared folder contains only files 1) that are in the public domain, 2) for which you have permission to share, or 3) that are made available under pro-sharing licenses, such as the Creative Commons license or other open media licenses [. . .].

While I would welcome (at least for purposes of illustration) a peer-to-peer client that delivered *only* files that met one of these three criteria, my suspicion is that the general public and the EFF would be disappointed by the aggregate content in such a network.

Figure 7. The EFF's campaign in support of "File-Sharing." Copyright © 2003, Electronic Frontier Foundation.

I'll examine the likely scope of available content for each of these classes of "sharable" files in turn.

Public Domain Files. The overarching effect of the Sonny Bono Copyright Term Extension Act of 1999 was the addition of 20 years to all extant and future copyright terms. This halted the movement of works from 1923 forward into the public domain. So the peer-to-peer client that adhered to the EFF's guidelines would primarily feature music from before 1923. This music would stretch from Thomas Edison's 1877 recording of "Mary Had a Little Lamb" to Al Jolson's 1922 recording of "Toot, Toot, Tootsie! (Good-Bye)" and for subsequent years feature only that music where through oversight or lack of interest, copyrights were not renewed.

Files For Which You Have Permission to Share. While some musicians have made an occasional song available without restricting its circulation or distribution, these cases are altogether rare. More commonly, some strings are attached to the distribution. While the band Wilco is celebrated for having made the whole of its album "Yankee Hotel Foxtrot" available via the Web while the band's label, weighed (at great length) whether the record should be released. Wilco's album was available only via streaming media, and peer-to-peer transfers of MP3 files of the "Yankee Hotel Foxtrot" songs were not authorized by the band or the label (Nonesuch) that ultimately released the album. Similarly, while Wilco made MP3 files of a follow-up EP available via the Web, visitors to the band's website were required to enter a code found within the "Yankee Hotel Foxtrot" CD packaging to access the MP3s. Wilco is rightly celebrated for pursuing innovative approaches to distribution of its music via the Internet. But while the public perception is that Wilco has put a lot of music "on the Web," the reality is that none of the above-cited files could fairly be uploaded to a peer-to-peer client that honored the EFF's above-cited criteria. Wilco's generosity, while considerable, does not extend all the way to general permission to circulate its music. And this approach is both common and understandable among acts with any significant commercial viability.

Files That Are Made Available Under Pro-Sharing License Like Creative Commons Licenses. There is now a growing body of material (estimated at over 50 million files of all types) now circulating under Creative Commons licenses. Most, but not all of the CC licenses would permit distribution via a peer-to-peer network. There is considerable potential for musicians and others to build audiences by releasing material without restriction. But we have yet to witness a song achieving general popularity (as measured by, say, the Billboard charts) while being distributed freely under a Creative Commons license. Lawrence Lessig's *Free Culture* demonstrated that a *book* released simultaneously as a free and largely unrestricted computer file would still sell. Adhering to the EFF's standard would mean that a peer-to-peer network could feature tracks like the Beastie Boys' "Now Get Busy," which was released as part of WIRED magazine's November 2004 compilation of tracks distributed under Creative Commons licenses. The disc's subtitle, "Rip.

Sample. Mash. Share." constitutes an open invitation for purchasers to upload the files to peer-to-peer services.

Taken together, there is considerable work that *could* be made available via peer-to-peer networks that is public domain, permitted, or licensed via Creative Commons and its analogs. But this is not what most peer-to-peer users are choosing to distribute (or inadvertently distributing).

In August of 2005, less than a year after the initial release of "Now Get Busy" I logged on to Limewire to see how many copies of the song were available as a rough index of the song's popularity among downloaders. This method is of only limited value, as the number of songs available can ebb and flow as users log on and off the service. Additionally, one is only able to determine the number of *uploaders* offering a song at a particular point in time. There is no necessary correspondence between the number of files offered and the number of files ultimately downloaded, because (as stated earlier) many users disable their shared folders. Nevertheless, the results of my brief survey of song availability provide at least a suggestion of degrees of demand for particular songs. The Beastie Boys' song—featuring both a Creative Commons license and a title that reinforces the WIRED CD's general invitation to share and remix—was available from a respectable nineteen uploaders. A representative public domain track, Jolson's "Toot-Toot, Tootsie!" was available from six. Works distributed with express permission from the musician, but *not* a Creative Commons license, are hard to come by, but a former member of Wilco, Jay Bennett, had three MP3 downloads available at his website. Bennett's website featured no notice or indication of the terms under which the files were being distributed, and a visitor could infer (rightly or wrongly) that neither Bennett nor his record company would object to further distribution of the songs via peer-to-peer networks. Even so, there was no trace of any of the three Bennett MP3s on Limewire when I searched. Admittedly, given the availability of the songs on the website, there is little incentive for any one user to take the initiative to further distribute the songs.

This brief canvass offers a snapshot of what peer-to-peer adhering to the EFF's guidelines might look like.

Meanwhile, Limewire's uploaders were offering hundreds of copies of expressly commercial files for which no permissions of any kind have been granted. Sheryl Crow, a vocal critic of unauthorized peer-to-peer downloads, had a 2004 chart single with her cover of Cat Stevens's "The First Cut is the Deepest." The Crow track was available from over 300 uploaders. The band most associated with opposition to unauthorized downloads, Metallica, also remains popular among Limewire's users. Over 200 uploaders were offering MP3s of the song ". . . And Justice For All." These uploads are occurring in spite of clear and unequivocal opposition from both the artists involved and the music companies to whom the artists sold their copyrights.

There are circumstances in which it might be considered reasonable or ethical to distribute music files without permission. But the nature of peer-to-peer distribution is such that files made available for a particular, and arguably ethical, reason are also available to all of the individuals on a given network. And there is no way to ensure that all of the uses of a given file are fair uses, *de minimis* uses, or otherwise ethical exceptions to copyright. In this context, the decision to override an artist's or copyright holder's stated objections to peer-to-peer distribution, if intended as a form of protest or political action, carries with it an obligation to state forthrightly and publicly the rationale for the distribution, and, in the grand tradition of the best civil disobedience, to be prepared to accept the consequences for one's actions, even if the laws involved might be unjust.

At present, however, the bulk of the Internet-based distribution of MP3 files occurs anonymously, with no interaction or conversation between the people whose computers are engaging in peer-to-peer transfers. There are many terms we might use to fairly and accurately describe these distributions.

"Sharing" ought not be among them.

6 Peer-to-Peer as Combat

There is a sad progression to the charges directed against peer-to-peer file transfers by the leaders of the content industries. When Napster brought peer-to-peer technology into the mainstream, it was attacked as an extension of the suspect and criminal exploits of hackers. Because *trespass* is the core of this charge, the content industries next focused on repositioning peer-to-peer transfers as theft, with "shoplifting" routinely cited as the best available parallel. "Theft" in turn, gave way to an expansionist recasting of "piracy." The term was detached from its conventional association with counterfeit goods, and deployed repeatedly to reinforce the notion that peer-to-peer users were pillaging the music and film industries. Once the implicit violence embedded in the piracy analogy took root, the stage was set for the ultimate rhetorical gambit: the equation of peer-to-peer technologies with warfare.

In a January 2002 *New York Times* article, Jack Valenti, then President of the Motion Picture Association of America (MPAA), likened his organization's efforts in opposing peer-to-peer downloads of motion pictures via the Internet to a military engagement. Valenti said, "We're fighting our own terrorist war," adding, "the great moat that protects us, and it is only temporary, is lack of broadband access" (Harmon).

Valenti's remarks position the film industry as both a victim and a target, and span centuries of military history. The timing of Valenti's comments makes it clear that his reference to a "terrorist war" was meant to be understood in the context of the U.S.'s response to the September 11, 2001, attacks on the World Trade Center and the Pentagon. Valenti was inviting readers of a newspaper serving the city hardest hit by these attacks to understand the film industry as having endured a parallel trauma. By contrast, Valenti's description of the industry as temporarily protected by a "great moat" positions the MPAA as, at best, a medieval protectorate, and at worst, the sort of plutocratic castle-keep regularly targeted by Robin Hood and his Merry Men.

Valenti's remarks are especially striking given the remarkable success the film industry was experiencing at roughly the same time he was speaking. For the U.S. motion picture industry, the 2002 Memorial Day holiday weekend was among the most lucrative in history. American moviegoers stampeded box offices, spending over $200 million on admissions. In June, 2002, *Business Week Online* reported that "box office receipts are 21 percent ahead of last year's pace" (Grover). By any reasonable measure, the film industry was in the midst of a very good year.

But Jack Valenti was not happy. According to the Boston-based "digital solutions" corporation Viant, 2002's 21 percent increase in box office receipts was counterbalanced by a 20 percent rise in illicit downloads of films, with roughly half a million copies downloaded each day (Chmielewski). These statistics prompted Valenti to observe, "It's getting clear—alarmingly clear, I might add—that we are in the midst of the possibility of Armageddon." Valenti continued: "Eight out of 10 [movies] have to go to airlines, to hotels, to Blockbuster, to HBO, then to basic cable—to get their money back. If you are ambushed in the early days of your theatrical exhibition, the chances of you recouping in a world that is mostly broadband would be very, very different" (Chmielewski).

Valenti's "Armageddon" is thus understandable as a "mostly broadband" world in which secondary and tertiary revenue streams for Hollywood films are threatened by unauthorized Internet-enabled downloads. These comments reflect a loss of perspective all too common in Hollywood. But Valenti's biography reveals that he has more than a passing acquaintance with the kind of apocalyptic threat his language trivializes.

Valenti is a decorated veteran of the Second World War. He was a close associate of Lyndon Johnson, and served that President as the U.S. ramped up its involvement in the Vietnam War. In short, prior to Valenti's assumption of the MPAA Presidency in 1966, he was a true Cold Warrior, writing and supervising the bulk of Johnson's speeches. He likely played a key role in the Johnson administration's withering attack on Barry Goldwater, the 1964 Republican nominee for U.S. President. Goldwater had a well-earned reputation as a hard right-winger, once defending himself by claiming that "extremism in the defense of liberty is no vice." Valenti seized on this, arguing behind closed doors that "we ought to treat Goldwater not as an equal, who has credentials to be president, but as a radical, a preposterous candidate who would ruin this country and our future" (Gould).

Valenti's successful deployment of this argument is testified to by the "Daisy" television commercial, in which the image of a small girl counting daisy petals is supplanted by the countdown to the launch of an intercontinental ballistic missile and scenes of apparent nuclear devastation. Without directly naming Goldwater, Johnson's voice intones: "These are the stakes. To make a world in which all of God's children can live, or to go into the darkness. We must either love each other, or we must die." Thus, the commercial expressly equated a vote for Goldwater with a vote for nuclear conflict, and four decades later it stands as one of the most questionable and extreme advertisements in the often sordid history of American political rhetoric. The Daisy commercial aired only once during the 1964 Presidential campaign, but it is generally understood to have had a devastating effect on the Goldwater campaign.

Given Valenti's experience as an architect of Johnson's most extreme media messages, Valenti's invocation of "Armageddon" should almost certainly be seen as a calculated statement from a man familiar with the particularities of both public speaking and political conflict. Even so, it remains tempting to dismiss Valenti's statements as rhetorical excesses of a man predisposed to hyperbole. Valenti did, after all, claim in 1983 that "the VCR is to the American film producer and the American public as the Boston strangler is to the woman home alone" in sworn testimony before the U.S. Senate (qtd. in Wu). But Valenti's rhetorical performances are far from anomalous in the ongoing debates over peer-to-peer downloads, in which the use and transmission of copyrighted materials are often recast as tactical warfare.

This chapter offers critical analysis of recent discourse on peer-to-peer file transfers, illustrating the degree to which participants in the debates over the legality of Napster and its successors position themselves as combatants. Further, this chapter maps this debate against the model of the Cold War (a model expressly invoked by Valenti and other participants in the debate) in part to point up how distant copyright questions are from actual warfare, and partly to illuminate the relative immaturity of the peer-to-peer debates. This point is underscored when the peer-to-peer debate is evaluated in terms of stasis theory, a classical rhetorical technique that, despite its vintage, provides a specific diagnosis for the impoverished discourse that has, to date, characterized this important public policy debate.

Since the advent of Napster, the content industries have grown increasingly comfortable with positioning peer-to-peer transfers as acts of war. Napter's arrival prompted a wave of rhetoric notable for its aggressively militaristic tone. In August 2000 Sony vice-president Steve Heckler mobilized a rhetorical gear which Trevor Merriden, author of the Napster history *Irresistible Forces,* properly describes as "almost Churchillian." Heckler stated:

> The industry will take whatever steps it needs to protect itself and protect its revenue streams. It will not lose that revenue stream, no matter what. [. . .] We will develop technology that transcends the individual user. We will firewall Napster at its source—we will block it at your cable company, we will block it at your phone company, we will block it at your ISP. We will firewall it at your PC. (qtd. in Merriden 35)

Indeed, Merriden is understating his case by describing Heckler's verbiage as *almost* Churchillian. Heckler's presentation is *expressly* Churchillian, in that it effectively parodies a specific Churchill speech from 1940—routinely cited as an exemplary use of the rhetorical device of *anaphora*—in which Churchill famously declared his opposition to the threat posed by Hitler's armies: "We shall fight on the beaches. We shall fight on the landing grounds. We shall fight in the fields, and in the streets, we shall fight in the hills." To the extent that Heckler's language invites comparison with Churchill's, Heckler should be understood to be tacitly linking those he would describe as intellectual property pirates with Nazis.

Warner Music executive Edgar Bronfman struck a similarly extreme tone when he argued, "If intellectual property is not protected—across the board, in every case, with no exceptions and no sophistry about a changing world—what will happen? Intellectual property will suffer the fate of the Buffalo" (qtd. in Alderman, *Sonic* 139). Bronfman is here proposing a standard that is both impossible and impractical. The U.S. no longer has notice or registration requirements, so, in effect, everything is copyrighted once it is fixed in a tangible form of expression. And U.S. courts have expressly ruled that digital media are "tangible" enough to establish "fixity." So every e-mail message, every Web page, every completed scrap of information, digital or printed, is copyrighted—and presumably subject to Bronfman's call for protection "across the board, in every case, with no exceptions." Bronfman's suggestion that without this maximal protection, intellectual property will tilt toward extinction is, in a word, absurd.

Intellectual property is a thriving industry in the U.S. According to recent estimates, the copyright industries account for roughly six percent of the U.S. gross domestic product, up from five percent in 2002. Clearly, intellectual property industries have thrived in the absence of the kinds of maximal protection Bronfman seeks. Nevertheless Bronfman proposed to counter his specious claims of the threat of extinction with his own program of extermination: "I am warring against the culture of the Internet, threatening to depopulate Silicon Valley as I move a Roman legion of Wall Street lawyers to litigate in Bellevue and San Jose" (qtd. in Alderman 139).

The above-cited examples of extreme rhetoric have all been drawn from opponents of peer-to-peer file exchanges, but peer-to-peer purveyors and enthusiasts are also implicated in the violent and militaristic rhetoric that too often characterizes these debates. In testimony delivered before the U.S. Senate, Napster CEO Hank Barry wrapped his defenses of his company in repeated descriptions of the software as heralding a vaguely defined "revolution." Barry first positions Napster inventor Shawn Fanning as a liberator: "Shawn Fanning began a revolution that is returning the Internet to its roots. [. . .] Napster does not copy files. It does not provide the technology for copying files. Napster does not make MP3 files. It does not transfer files" (Barry). But Barry's attempts to reposition Napster as an essentially innocuous technology are undermined by Barry's insistence on positioning Napster as marking a breaking point: "Napster simply facilitates communication among people interested in music. It is a return to the original information sharing approach of the Internet, allowing for a depth and a scale of information that is truly revolutionary" (Barry). "Revolutionary" is, of course, a term that, in and of itself, constitutes effective marketing of any Internet-directed product, and Barry's usage of the term should be understood as an attempt to establish novelty and primacy for Napster. But the language of revolution also carries with it an unmistakable threat to an established order.

As the debate between Napster and the major labels heated up, Napster enthusiasts took up their own rhetorical weaponry in order to join Barry's purported "revolution." On a Web site featuring the rallying cry, "Fight RIAA—Let's Get Those Bastards," we see Hank Barry's rhetoric echoed in the site creator's choice of "Live Free or Die"—a phrase now synonymous with the American Revolution.

Figure 8. The logo for an anti-RIAA site; note the use of "Live Free or Die!" Copyright © 2001, L. Anderson.

The implicit argument of this site is that the RIAA is to Napster users as King George III and the British were to the Yankee colonists. We do well to recall, at least momentarily, that the Declaration of Independence indicts George III as follows:

> He has plundered our seas, ravaged our Coasts, burnt our towns, and destroyed the lives of our people.
>
> He is at this time transporting large Armies of foreign Mercenaries to compleat the works of death, desolation and tyranny, already begun with circumstances of Cruelty and perfidy scarcely paralleled in the most barbarous ages, and totally unworthy the Head of a civilized nation.

While overpriced compact discs and outrageously one-sided recording contracts can and should prompt sharp criticism, the Fight-RIAA site's hyperbolic characterizations of the conflict between peer-to-peer "colonists" and the "tyrant" RIAA undermine efforts to engage with peer-to-peer technologies in their rich complexity.

A contemporaneous hacker site is even more violent in its rhetoric, headlining itself "Kill the RIAA." The site promotes a code-based protocol for direct artist-to-fan distribution. While welling up from within hacker culture, this proposal is fairly benign. It involves extension of code for MP3 files to facilitate listeners making direct contributions to the music's creators, thereby cutting the RIAA and similar copyright holders out of the exchange, and eventually "killing" them.

Figure 9: The "Kill the RIAA" Protocol.

The hacker's attempt to develop a protocol which would, in effect, eliminate the need for the RIAA is grounded in a utopian vision. The impulse driving the hacker's discussion is a probably naïve presumption that the development of an effective code-based payment mechanism would be able to transform the existing music industry into something like "shareware," in which satisfied users of freely distributed software choose, on a voluntary basis, to compensate software developers. Unfortunately, this utopian vision is counterbalanced by the violence of the hacker's rhetoric. Over the course of this discussion, the emphasis on a positive exchange between artists and fans is at odds with the "killing" invoked to set the stage. And the RIAA is consistently positioned as an enemy combatant, foreclosing the possibility of negotiation or cooperation. The hacker's attempts to find a code-based means of bringing the RIAA to its knees suggest an "arms race" of sorts, playing out in cyberspaces where music files are circulating.

As the RIAA ramped up its criticism of Napster, the war metaphor became increasingly common. In a February 2000 exchange on Slashdot, we see correspondents debating whether a particular Cold War era model ought to be applied to their circumstances. A correspondent going by "Rader" begins the exchange by observing:

> RADER: We are possibly watching the breakup of a major cartel. My parents had Vietnam. I've got the dawning of the digital age. A digital world impacting huge corporations that spend 200 million dollars a year just in legal expenses. Why does Napster get more bad publicity than the PROOF of the Big-5 [the five largest record companies] collaborating and setting illegal prices in stores? Proof that Bo Didley [sic] has no money to his name, yet created Rock & Roll?
>
> Maybe I'm the guy who ran to Canada instead of going to Vietnam, and you're the ROTC punk who thinks it's your duty to go to war. Whichever was right or wrong, it's still a controversy today, much like this issue could possibly be.

Rader's comments are, at first blush, not particularly coherent or persuasive. Rader's strongest argument is that the core allegations lodged in an ultimately successful class action lawsuit against the RIAA for price fixing had been under-reported. Rader's argument was borne out in part when, in 2004, the five major record labels paid out $67.4 million and $75.7 million worth of CDs to settle the case. But ultimately Rader's argument devolves to an allegation that there is an imbalance in the public criticism of disreputable behavior by both record companies and music consumers. Later, it is not clear whether Rader means for the "breakup of [the] major cartel," or the "dawn of the digital age" to serve as the basis for his comparison to Vietnam. That said, Rader does demonstrate some understanding of the history of the Vietnam era, and allies himself with the so-called "draft dodgers" while lambasting another correspondent for, in effect, being a government dupe, much as military volunteers and conscripts were sometimes criticized in the late 1960s and early 1970s.

But the carelessness with which Rader draws this analogy prompted an incredulous response from another Slashdot correspondent:

> ZIKZAK: Holy shit! Are you really claiming that the battle over MP3 pirating could be equivalent in importance to the Vietnam War? Fuck, I have now seen the absolute pinnacle of pathetic justification. Equating the slightly over-priced and admittedly greedy recording industry's practices to the death of thousands and thousands of young men is absolutely the lowest thing I've ever seen on slashdot.
>
> Congratulations. You have scraped absolute bottom.

Zikzak's outburst prompted what appeared to be an embarrassed silence from Rader, and other participants, in what had, to that point, been a lively discussion. Eventually another participant in the discussion rose up to defend Rader's analogy:

> WAH: Well, there's at least one part of the analogy that holds. Both are (were) being drawn up as a fight against communism (while the reality is (was) much less drastic). And if the laws we have here in the U.S. were universally enforced, you would have about 30 million people in jail for *their entire lifetime*. Some people are just trying to avoid another catastrophe, over-the-top analogies (as this is) are one way to make the direction we are currently headed (unwinnable war with massive loss of life(time) looming) clear.

Wah's post features a link to a legal website that houses Chapter 12 of Title 17 of the United States Code, in which the substantial penalties established by the Digital Millennium Copyright Act are outlined. The Act specifies penalties of up to $1,000,000 and ten years in prison for those who circumvent copyright protection measures. Wah's estimate of thirty million in prison is highly questionable. Most Americans have neither the interest nor the technical skill needed to circumvent copyright protection systems. But within the context of Slashdot's discussion over whether the Napster debate parallels Vietnam, Wah's post draws a link between the conscientious objectors and draft dodgers imprisoned during the Vietnam era, and the potential prisoners who, in Wah's estimation, conscientiously object to or "dodge" copyright protection in virtual spaces.

The positioning of peer-to-peer transfers and their attendant debates as acts of war are becoming increasingly codified. Litman's 2002 article "War Stories," features a conclusion in which she flatly equates the peer-to-peer debates with warfare:

> Commercial content owners (and their copyright lawyers) believe they are in a war for their own survival, and are committing extraordinary resources to ensure that they emerge victorious. They are fighting the copyright wars using all of the public relations tools at their disposal. They are fielding armies of copyright lobbyists and making campaign contributions so substantial that members of Congress have started to wage turf battles of their own to get jurisdiction over copyright legislation.

Litman is an astute critic of the copyright lobby, and her work as a whole points up the degree to which the public's interest has been compromised by recent shifts in copyright law. Litman's "Choosing Metaphors" chapter in *Digital Copyright* offers a sustained examination of the degree to which copyright policy has been influenced by a variety of suspect metaphoric constructions. And yet, the war metaphor is so entrenched that Litman here invokes it to frame her discussion despite her certain recognition of the profound distance between copyright violations and combat. We do well to ask why this metaphor has proven so resilient, persisting even as video and Internet-circulated images of the second U.S.-led war in Iraq offered a jarring reminder of the horrific consequences of military conflict.

While participants in the peer-to-peer debate from all sides of the issue routinely pursue analogies drawn from across centuries of military history, the most common comparisons remain those which repurpose the language and history of the Cold War (and of Vietnam, the paradigmatic "little war" within the bloated corpus of the Cold War). These comparisons grossly inflate the stakes of the debate. As Zikzak's eruption rightly reminds us, there is no body count associated with peer-to-peer file transmission. Whatever the costs associated with "illegal" downloading might be, they pale before the awful human toll of Vietnam and the Cold War. Why then does the analogy prove irresistible to participants in this debate? The answer is, in part, that there are a number of *superficial* similarities between the history of the Cold War and the history of the peer-to-peer debates.

Historians typically date the Cold War as stretching from roughly 1947 to 1989. Most accounts point to the Cold War commencing during a brutal winter in Europe, which ratcheted up a contest between the U.S. and the Soviet Union over which country could provide more aid to the affected nations (most of which were already reeling from the after-effects of World War II). There is near-universal agreement that the Cold War ended with the fall of the Berlin Wall on November 9, 1989. While various labels are applied to the intervening periods, there is general agreement that the U.S. and the Soviet Union engaged in a pitched conflict with the very real possibility of nuclear confrontation after reaching a point of schism in the late 1940s. This nuclear threat persisted until the inauguration of a mutually acknowledged period of détente in 1968.

For years, no one was certain how close the two superpowers had come to what was then referred to as a "tactical nuclear exchange." But a recent conference on the 40th Anniversary of the Cuban Missile Crisis pointed up how real the danger had been. The *New York Times's* coverage of the conference contained a harrowing account of the peak of the crisis, in which a Soviet submarine commander, responding to depth charges dropped by an American destroyer, ordered the preparation of the submarine's nuclear torpedo. The *Times* report quotes the commander as having said: "Maybe the war has already started up there, while we are doing somersaults here! [. . .] We're going to blast them now! We will die, but we will sink them all. We will not disgrace our navy!" (Gonzalez) The Cuban Missile Crisis functions as a generally recognized "flashpoint" within the history of the Cold War. It is the point at which the confrontation between the then-extant superpowers was most pitched, most pointed, and potentially, most destructive.

Within the context of the peer-to-peer debates, the showdown between the RIAA and Napster that culminated in the injunction that closed Napster parallels the Cuban Missile Crisis, featuring similarly intransigent parties mixing secret tactical exchanges with aggressive public posturing. Like the Missile Crisis, the peer-to-peer debate prompted high-level government hearings, with representatives from the parties concerned campaigning to earn comparisons to Adlai Stevenson, who famously unveiled the "smoking gun" photographs of Soviet military installations in Cuba in October 1962 United Nations hearings.

Surprisingly, Metallica drummer Lars Ulrich's testimony has come to be regarded as the parallel rhetorical "flashpoint" within the peer-to-peer debate. Ulrich's arguments, cited repeatedly in this book, neatly encapsulate the array of arguments promoted by the content industries. Further, Ulrich managed to successfully negotiate the high drama of the superficially absurd proceedings, and speak in a way that prompted sustained discussions among all parties to the debate.

Ulrich closed his testimony by quoting New York *Times* columnist Edward Rothstein, who, in an essay entitled "Swashbuckling Anarchists Try to Eliminate Copyright from Cyberspace," wrote:

> Information doesn't want to be free; only the transmission of information wants to be free. Information, like culture, is the result of a labor and devotion, investment and risk; it has a value. And nothing will lead to a more deafening cultural silence than ignoring that value and celebrating "the near perfect anarchy" of Freenet and Napster running amok.

Ulrich subtly revised Rothstein, adjusting the final sentences to read "celebrating . . . [companies like] Napster," suggesting that, as a member of a band that foregrounds its anti-authoritarian, oppositional stance, Ulrich was uncomfortable with the positioning of the debate as a dispute between "investors" on his side of the argument, and "anarchists" as his opponents. Indeed, Metallica's sharply critical assessment of the status quo on records like *And Justice For All* made the band an especially unlikely ally for the record industry. Yet by citing Rothstein's essay, Ulrich trafficked in Rothstein's polarizing rhetoric, which positioned Napster and similar programs as cultural doomsday devices.

It remains important to recall that the question addressed by the U.S. Senate hearings on peer-to-peer was ultimately nothing more than whether the RIAA or Napster (or, perhaps, both) would ultimately profit from peer-to-peer file transfers. Further, while the peer-to-peer debates spiraled from courtrooms to the court of public opinion, all of the parties involved agreed to respect the will of U.S. judges and legislative bodies.

With the parallels between "flashpoint" confrontations in place, an extended chronology for Cold War comparisons can be established. The roots of the peer-to-peer debates can be traced back to the record industry's shift from the 45 rpm vinyl single to the long playing album, followed by attempted shifts to reel-to-reel, 8-track tape, cassette, and, ultimately, the successful replacement of vinyl with the compact disc. The near-elimination of the single as a medium effectively required music consumers to purchase entire albums to secure copies of the individual songs they favored. And the introduction of four "long-playing" formats in a quarter century (each touted as superior to its predecessor) prompted many consumers to purchase their favorite music on as many as four different media. Prior to Napster, music consumers had become understandably wary of the record industry, and increasingly critical of the high prices of compact discs. The settlement agreement in the price-fixing case referenced by Rader was all the evidence many consumers needed of the music industry's bad faith. And this was compounded when the record companies in the settlement complied in a desultory fashion with an order to supplement the suit's mandatory financial settlement with donations of compact discs to libraries. A 2004 *USA Today* article suggests that that the companies involved complied with the letter, but not the spirit of the settlement:

> [T]he shipments included many unpopular titles that library officials wouldn't have chosen for their collections. And other usable titles arrived in such quantity that the supply will exceed demand.
>
> "These are old materials, unpopular materials the companies had left over," said Lynda Murray, director of government relations for the Ohio Library Council. "For the most part, these are CDs that libraries would have never purchased or included in their collections."
>
> For example, in suburban Worthington, the libraries' take included 19 copies of *The Mystery of Santo Domingo De Silos*, an album of Gregorian

chants, while suburban Bexley Public Library employees found in their shipment 15 copies of Whitney Houston's 1991 recording of The Star Spangled Banner. ("Free Compact Discs")

The record industry has, in some circumstances, shown itself to be remarkably tone-deaf with respect to the consequences of its actions. Few industries are more widely loathed by their customer base. And the distaste many music consumers voice for the record industry is compounded by the complaints of working musicians.

Five years before Napster, musician and producer Steve Albini wrote a scathing essay entitled "The Problem With Music," in which he documented how a successful major-label record release would net its record company over $700,000, while the members of the band responsible for the record would receive less than $5,000 each. As Napster gained steam, rocker Courtney Love gave a speech, later published as "Courtney Love Does the Math" where she offered a similar financial analysis, with a band grossing $11 million, but ending up with "zero." Love observes: "The system's set up so almost nobody gets paid" (Love). With these complaints circulating and meshing with high CD prices throughout the 1990s, it seems clear that if Napster hadn't offered an avenue for music consumers to lash back at the record companies, another similar "flashpoint" would have materialized. While the slow-burning narrative of consumer dissatisfaction with the record industry does not offer the relatively sharp schism of the Cold War, it does provide a portrait of escalating hostilities setting the stage for a dramatic confrontation in which one side is ultimately forced to "stand down."

The period immediately following the Napster "crisis," recalled the pitched period in the 1960s when the U.S. and the Soviet Union heated up the nuclear rhetoric while confining themselves to indirect confrontations via espionage and "little wars" against small nations positioned as emblematic of "the enemy." Skirmishes between the record industry (and industry-supporting performers) and file-traders became increasingly common, and some of these battles had the jittery energy of the spy culture celebrated in the wake of the Cuban Missile Crisis.

In 2003, Madonna, fresh from having recorded the theme for the latest installment in the James Bond series, completed an album entitled *American Life* to surround the Bond theme (formally listed on the album as "'Die Another Day' from the MGM motion picture *Die Another Day*"). In coordination with the Warner Music Group, Madonna recorded a profane challenge to downloaders (she snarls "what the fuck do you think you're doing?") which was then disguised as leaked tracks from the *American Life* album, and uploaded onto the major file-transfer systems that rose up in Napster's wake (e.g., Kazaa, Limewire). By flooding these networks with bogus files, Warner and Madonna hoped to at least slow, and perhaps impede altogether the traffic in *American Life* downloads. Shortly after the bogus files were uploaded, a hacker cracked Madonna's site and posted a parodic response ("This is what the fuck I think I'm doing") followed by five genuine music files from *American Life*. In addition to the hack, the Madonna soundclip became the focus of "The Madonna Remix Project" with dozens of downloaders preparing musical compositions featuring the snippet, usually mixed in with fierce and/or hilarious attacks on Madonna and Warner Music Group.

The following year, the RIAA acknowledged that it had undertaken a broader campaign of larding peer-to-peer networks with bogus files. While these files featured artists' names and song titles, and appeared to be MP3 files of appropriate size and length, downloaders would hear only static or silence, or sometimes a recording warning against "illegal downloading." In response, the P2P company Altnet sued the RIAA for violating Altnet's patent on an algorithm used by the company to "properly" identify MP3 files.

Thus, as in the middle stages of the Cold War, the "official" political actions of the competing parties are underscored by waves of secret, often anonymous activity directed at technologically undermining the opposition. As with their Cold War predecessors, all parties concerned appear to find this approach preferable to the "hot war" alternative. But my ultimate goal in this review of the superficial similarities between the Cold War and the history of peer-to-peer file transfers is not merely to find the right sort of war to function as an analogy for this ongoing debate. Indeed, the acceptance of war as metaphor gives away too much of the game for those who hope for expanded opportunities for peer-to-peer exchanges because it accepts military conflicts over real property as exemplary.

Law professor Dan Burk has pointedly and persistently argued against the impulse to simply "port" law from terrestrial spaces to their supposed cyberspace counterparts. As early as 1997, Burk recognized, rightly, that there is "no coherent homology between cyberspace and real space," and that the real space analogies routinely deployed to explain cyberspaces were likely obscuring at least as much as they illuminated about the Internet. In a similar vein, I argue here that the physical realities of terrestrial war (whether hot or cold) are absolutely removed from disagreements over even the wholesale appropriation of intellectual property. Recourse to war as the metaphoric frame for the debate obscures the degree to which peer-to-peer exchanges complement and extend pre-computer modes of distributing and exchanging information.

The corrupted status of much of the rhetoric surrounding peer-to-peer exchanges is thrown into sharp relief by even ancient tools for understanding arguments. Though initially developed as an inventional technique for ancient Greek courts, the stasis theory advanced by Hermagoras of Temnos in the second century BCE. offers a powerful diagnosis of the disconnections in the peer-to-peer debates. Hermagoras's theory offers four focus points (conjecture, definition, quality, and policy) as a means of tracing whether parties to an argument have identified the true source of their conflict. Janet Davis describes the process as follows:

> The rhetor proceeds through a prescribed series of dichotomizing questions to locate and identify the unresolved matter. Locating the stasis within the system presents the rhetor with not only a name for the category of argument but also a recommended strategy for pursuing it. (693)

As Jeanne Fahnestock and Marie Secor have pointed out, Hermagoras's questions are presented in hierarchical order. They observe:

> Questions of fact or conjecture in the first stasis are prior to those of definition in the second; definitions in turn must be established before the quality is debated; and finally all three must be answered or assumed before an action can be recommended or taken in a specific case. (137)

Thus, according to first step in the stasis process, parties must arrive at an agreement that a specific act is occurring or has occurred. In the peer-to-peer debates, it seems clear that all parties involved would agree that peer-to-peer transfers of copyright-protected materials have occurred and will continue to occur via peer-to-peer systems, so stasis has been achieved with respect to questions of conjecture. Having established that a particular act has occurred and is occurring, we move to the second stasis.

The second stasis is the stasis of definition. Sharon Crowley and Debra Hawhee identify "How can the act be defined?" and "What kind of thing or event is it?" as core questions for the second stasis (47, 50). These questions foreground the fault lines in the ongoing debates with absolute clarity. The content industries have to a great degree shaped this debate in apocalyptic terms, with peer-to-peer exchanges positioned as at best failures of will, more typically as examples of hacking, theft, piracy, or war. As suggested by the examples above, even peer-to-peer advocates have too often accepted these terms. Current references to peer-to-peer transfers as "file sharing" more accurately reflect the sentiments of the many communities taking advantage of peer-to-peer networks. But this usage is grounded in a knowing refusal to engage with the complex ethical questions surrounding the unauthorized sharing of non-rivalrous, readily reproducible digital files.

The peer-to-peer debate is clearly stalled at the second stasis. The definitions used by the participants in the debate are so distant and so distorted that it is sometimes difficult to recognize that the act of transferring files between computers is, in and of itself, common, unremarkable, and morally neutral. While stasis theory advises participants in a debate to defer questions of policy until both the definition and the quality of an action are understood, the current debate has vaulted the second and third stases. The U.S. Congress is now actively considering the policy questions without these definitions and evaluations having stabilized, and the consequence will almost certainly be continuing imbalance in intellectual property policies as they relate to peer-to-peer technologies.

Despite a wave of speculation in the wake of the RIAA lawsuits, suggesting that content industries and leading peer-to-peer companies might achieve something akin to *détente*, the "border skirmishes" continue unabated. The RIAA has settled comfortably into a roughly monthly pattern of announcing lawsuits against hundreds of peer-to-peer users.

So it was surprising when, on August 22, 2005, at an industry summit, Warner Music CEO Edgar Bronfman unilaterally stated that armistice had been achieved:

> [T]he war between the music companies and consumers has been fought. We lost. Okay? So, let's just move on. Which is to say, we've got to make our music available to people. We just need to be allowed to have a business model that allows copyright holders and owners to be compensated for their work. But our job is to get music to everyone, everywhere, as readily and as seamlessly as possible. (Bronfman)

Bronfman made this statement in the same month when the Japanese version of Apple's iTunes Music Store opened without songs from the catalogs of Sony and Bronfman's Warner Music Group because they were unable to agree on appropriate terms for the licenses. The typical share for the major labels on each 99 cent download is currently about 70 cents. According to the *New York Times* Sony and Warner favored eliminating Apple's fixed 99 cent pricing in favor of a variable pricing structure.

> [T]he one-price model that iTunes has adopted—99 cents to download any song—could be replaced with a more complex structure that prices songs by popularity. A hot new single, for example, could sell for $1.49, while a golden oldie could go for substantially less than 99 cents. (Leeds)

The iTunes Music Store is far and away the most successful retailer of online music, though subscription services like those offered by Rhapsody and Napster 2.0 appear to be making some inroads. Relative to the subscription services, Apple's sales of over 500,000,000 downloaded songs in the two-and-a-half years since its April, 2003 launch make a clear case for iTunes as the goose that is presently laying the golden eggs. The *Times* quoted one industry analyst who responded to the variable pricing proposal by suggesting that the music industry should leave well enough alone:

> "As I recall, three years ago these guys were wandering around with their hands out looking for some-

one to save them," said Mike McGuire, an analyst at Gartner G2. "It'd be rather silly to try to destabilize him because iTunes is one of the few bright spots in the industry right now. He's got something that's working." (Leeds)

The *Times* also referenced unnamed executives who had concluded that the proposal was at least untimely and probably unwise as well: "Music executives who support Mr. Jobs say the higher prices could backfire, sending iTunes' customers in search of songs on free, unauthorized file-swapping networks." Bronfman's purported cessation of hostilities did not appear to preclude second-guessing the price structure of the sole truly successful approach to online distribution of music.

At the same time, the *other* major content industry association, the MPAA, was pursuing the latest phases of its own lawsuit campaign. On August 25, 2005, the MPAA filed 286 lawsuits against users of peer-to-peer technologies. MPAA Senior Vice President John Malcom issued a statement, stating: "Internet movie thieves be warned: You have no friends in the online community when you are engaging in copyright theft" (MPAA, "Illegal Downloading"). The MPAA had also seized and shuttered a popular website named "LokiTorrent," that had offered streamlined connectivity to the BitTorrent peer-to-peer network, a major source for downloads of large files, including motion pictures and television programs. The MPAA posted a threatening notice to the site, warning LokiTorrent users that they could run, but not hide from prosecution.

The MPAA's LokiTorrent notice reflects the hyperbolic inaccuracies now all too common in the peer-to-peer debates. From the blustering headline to the flat equation of downloading with theft, the former LokiTorrent site reflects the continuing rhetoric of threat and hostility. For this reason, it was an obvious target for parody.

As the creators of the site entitled "The MPAA vs. An Army of Mice" clearly know, parody remains one of the most successful defenses against a charge of infringement. Indeed, the site's creators even included a link to the Parody Doctrine at the bottom of their page. One website approvingly citing the "Army of Mice" page refers to it as a "remix," thereby invoking a key term for those who seek broader access to copyrighted materials. Remixing is arguably the signature art form of the digital era. While the term stems from the practices of dub and

Figure 10: The warning posted by the MPAA to the former LokiTorrent site. Copyright © 2005, Motion Picture Association of America.

reggae mixmasters like Lee "Scratch" Perry, who created multiple versions of a basic music track, the concept has come to describe a broad array of cultural practices in a digital context. Digital media make the appropriation and recontextualization of snippets of culture remarkably easy. As with the above-cited Madonna Remix Project, when the content industries insult a broad swath of their core consumers, the response, more often then not, is for their own words to be sliced, diced, and reworked into a fierce counterpunch.

While it is tempting to simply celebrate the "Army of Mice" parody as the one of the latest examples of the virtual impossibility of containing creativity, the site's own rhetorical excesses position it as a saber-rattling tit-for-tat exchange in an ongoing race to the rhetorical bottom.

Figure 11: The ShutdownThis.com "Army of Mice" parody.

The site is on fairly solid footing when it complains about copyright laws being "distorted beyond their original intent" and also when it challenges the MPAA's flat equation of downloading as tangible theft. But when the site casts its lot with the goal of "den[ying] thousands of dishonest, lazy executives of their crack smoking livelihood," we are in the familiar rhetorical gutter of the baseless *ad hominem* attack, even when the language is likely intended as hyperbolic humor. Though the "Army of Mice" parody responds to the MPAA with creativity and wit, it also accepts and perpetuates the characterization of the peer-to-peer debates as a "war." While composed of "mice" the ShutdownThis website is still marshalling an "army."

The path to fair and appropriate policies addressing peer-to-peer technologies continues to be obscured by the polarizing rhetoric often used by the participants in the debate. The content industries have repeatedly attempted to position peer-to-peer technologies as weapons, and peer-to-peer users as criminals and terrorists. These arguments tend to conflate peer-to-peer technologies with the uses to which they are being put. While some of these uses are at least unethical and potentially illegal, many are not. The content industries' arguments to date threaten to disrupt growth and innovation in peer-to-peer technologies, which already offer computer users far more than free, easy access to the latest Top-40 hit. Peer-to-peer networks' true potential will only be realized once U.S. culture settles on a means of expediting the movement of cultural artifacts into the public domain. The content industries' continuing positioning of peer-to-peer as an assault on the producers of intellectual property will, inevitably, delay this realization.

Too often, those who seek a more principled discussion of the power and potential of peer-to-peer technologies accept and perpetuate the framing of the peer-to-peer debates as war. The consequences of the continuing hostilities now threaten, as is so often the case with warfare, to leave no possibility for a true "winner." In a 2005 speech, Litman sharply criticized the combatants:

> We are not going to be able to rebuild the law that we're destroying in this war without a great deal of compromise, many concessions, and a large dose of mutual trust, and we've just spent the past ten years proving to one another that we can't be trusted. There's a great deal of mistrust right now and it certainly looks to me as if most of it is richly deserved. There's been an inordinate amount of bullying and threats, a fair amount over-zealous advocacy on all sides that has sometimes crossed the line into bad faith litigation or deceptive lobbying. ("War and Peace")

Litman's language here echoes the Cold War threat of "mutually assured destruction," and even if the stakes of the copyright cold war are comparatively minor, the time has come for the combatants to stand down. Refusal to engage in the rhetoric of warfare is both a form of conscientious objection and a long overdue step on the path toward copyright policies tailored to the practical realities and the immense potential of digital media. The next step is the articulation of ethical stances that reflect the conscience implicit in the objection.

7 Conclusion: The Cat Came Back

Today, the striking iconography developed by the Napster corporation (including the impish headphone-wearing Napster "cat" logo) lives on as the public face of Napster 2.0, a pay-for-play music service offered by Roxio. But Napster 2.0 is demonstrably *not* Napster. Indeed, the Napster 2.0 pay-for-play service eliminates the community-building features (e.g., chat functionality among uploaders and downloaders) that made Napster both distinctive and especially efficient. And the licensing agreements that repositioned Napster on the safe side of the law give the lie to Napster's still anti-authoritarian advertising, in which the iconic cat momentarily appears as a metalhead, a gangsta rapper, or a stoned reggae fan. Napster 2.0 is struggling to find its way as a pay-for-play service. The cultural phenomenon of napsterization remains wild and on the loose. While Napster limited itself to music files, the latest generation of peer-to-peer clients is open to *anything* in digital form, leaving Napsters 1.0 and 2.0 looking tame by comparison.

The relative wildness of Napster's offspring has driven the increasingly pitched debates over the ethics and legality of peer-to-peer downloads to the point where the continuing availability and utility of the technology itself is by no means assured. (By this I mean *legal* availability. If we set aside potential shifts in the law, it is clear that peer-to-peer technologies will be forever with us. The efficiencies that can be achieved by leveraging peer-to-peer's economies of scale are just too irresistible now that the P2P cat is well out of the bag.) The increasing association of peer-to-peer technologies with criminality is especially worrisome because there is broad agreement across academic disciplines that peer-to-peer technologies are both a foundational structure and a critical element of the current Internet. In his 2001 book *Copyrights and Copywrongs,* Vaidhyanathan argues that peer-to-peer principles are embedded throughout the Internet:

> The Internet as originally conceived in the late 1960s was a peer-to-peer system. The goal of the original ARPANET was to share computing resources around the U.S. The challenge for this effort was to integrate different kinds of existing networks as well as future technologies with one common network that would allow every host to be an equal player[. . .]. The ARPANET connected them together not in a master/slave or client/server relationship, but rather as equal computing peers. (180)

Four years later, Vaidhyanathan's argument was underscored when a group of seventeen prominent computer science professors submitted an *amicus* brief to the U.S. Supreme Court in the high-profile case of *MGM v. Grokster*. The *Grokster* case centered on a post-Napster generation of peer-to-peer software that eliminated the central cataloging servers that ultimately proved Napster's undoing. Because Napster potentially *could* determine whether specific infringing files were listed on its servers, the company arguably had an obligation to block access to those files. The peer-to-peer companies enmeshed in *Grokster* sidestepped this issue by employing participants' computers to construct the catalog of available files. These companies argued that they had both no control over and no knowledge of the specific files transferred via their software. The seventeen computer scientists, writing in support of the peer-to-peer software companies, argued that "P2P networks are not new developments in network design, but rather the design on which the Internet itself is based" (Abelson, et al.) To the extent that the current debates over securing compensation for copyrighted materials effectively challenge the legality of peer-to-peer networks, they also challenge the legality of a significant portion of the Internet itself.

While much of the activity on the contemporary Internet might be described as client-server (and thus predicated on an imbalanced relationship between participants) there are also numerous sites within the Internet that depend on a roughly level relationship among participants. The most prominent example is the Usenet news groups (e.g., alt.music.no-depression) that prior to the advent of the World Wide Web, were, taken together, the most popular spaces on the Internet. Usenet is, to this day, a peer-to-peer application, with level relation-

Conclusion: The Cat Came Back

ships among the NNTP servers that store and forward articles to one another. Thus, the need for informed policies with regard to the use and circulation of copyrighted works is critical, not just for the United States, but in an international context, because *the Internet itself is (among other things) a peer-to-peer network.*

Nevertheless, countering the computer science professors' brief was a contemporaneous *New York Times* editorial, addressing the *Grokster* case, and egregiously entitled "When David Steals Goliath's Music." The *Times* editorial offers a clear indication of just how much was at stake in the Grokster case, and is at stake in the peer-to-peer debates. After commencing with a title that tacitly equates peer-to-peer technologies with theft, the *Times* editorial board concludes with this stunning argument:

> Grokster's supporters are justified in worrying that if the courts are too quick to rein in new technology, innovation can be stifled. They are also right to point out that copyright has sometimes been given too much protection, notably in the Copyright Term Extension Act, which gratuitously added 20 years to existing copyrights. But these concerns do not erase the continuing importance of intellectual property, which is unquestionably under assault.
>
> Both the court and Congress should be sensitive to evolving technologies. But they should not let technology evolve in a way that deprives people who create of the ability to be paid for their work. ("When David Steals")

Despite a paragraph ably documenting some of the more troubling recent shifts in intellectual property policy, the *Times* ultimately argues against "letting technology evolve" if that evolution might deprive intellectual property creators of "the ability to be paid for their work." Of course, technological innovation does just that *all the time.* The twentieth entury is replete with inventions, from the player piano to the VCR, each of which posed a significant threat to an existing structure of compensation for creative work. Yet the Constitutional clause that is the basis for U.S. copyright law announces the goal of "promot[ing] the progress of science and useful arts." That a newspaper with a reputation as strong as the *Times'* is now arguing that copyright effectively requires the suppression of technology is an indication of how far we have traveled from Thomas Jefferson's sensibilities. And I regret to say that my own disciplinary forebears in rhetoric and composition studies played a significant role in shaping our current circumstance, in which the "people who create" are often privileged to the point that technological development is stifled.

In 1996 article entitled "Intellectual Property and Composition Studies," Andrea Lunsford and Susan West offer a sharply critical assessment of their own discipline:

> [T]he teaching of writing has traditionally been invested in a model of composing that makes solitary reflection central to the production of "original" texts absolutely "owned" by their creators, a model of singular authorship and ownership perpetuated effectively by teachers of writing (and educational systems in general). [. . .] [A] vision of singular, stable authorship and autonomous creative acts has profoundly influenced copyright doctrine. (387)

Lunsford (along with another collaborator, Lisa Ede) had already challenged this model by identifying, acknowledging, and celebrating the degree to which many writers collaborate successfully and efficiently to produce written work. Lunsford's work dovetailed with work by many other scholars in rhetoric and composition who expressly critiqued the construct of the Romantic author—described by Martha Woodmansee as "solitary, originary, and proprietary"—as the necessary model for *all* writers. Especially notable among these scholars were Karen Burke LeFevre, whose 1986 book, *Invention as a Social Act,* pointed up the degree to which rhetorical invention is not the by-product of isolated individuals, but rather of participants in communicative networks; James E. Porter, whose 1984 *Rhetoric Review* article "Intertextuality and the Discourse Community" described the degree to which composers of texts depended upon and responded to their social contexts; and Gail Hawisher and Cynthia Selfe, who founded the journal *Computers and Composition* in 1983 and therein published dozens of articles addressing the profound implications of digital media for the practice of writing.

When Lunsford and West wrote "Intellectual Property and Composition Studies" they were certainly aware of the excellent work critiquing and challenging traditional approaches to the teaching of writing. But their conclusion was that the bulk of composition pedagogy was nevertheless directed at perpetuating the solitary author/owner as the preferred "model composer." Further, Lunsford and West saw this flawed pedagogical approach as having significant implications beyond the boundaries of the composition classroom: They wrote, "[I]t seems not too much of a stretch to read composition theories and pedagogies as deeply complicit in the expansion of copyright and the tilt towards a strong protectionist policy regarding "authorial" rights" (397). Indeed, composition classes are never merely about the production of written work. They are the spaces in which colleges and universities most directly address and model the creative process.

Composition classes are also among the first college-level classes where the politics and mechanics of using and appropriating others' work are points of focus. Composition classes routinely devote significant time and energy to teaching the proper use of quotations and scholarly citation practices. They are also the spaces within colleges and universities where instructors are most likely to devote more than a few minutes to the topic of plagiarism. For these reasons, composition classes have a profound influence on students' sense of their own actions as writers and producers of creative work. Composition classes are often the spaces in which students cultivate an informed understanding of how to navigate the boundaries between their own work and the work of others. The principles embedded in the pedagogies of composition classrooms are likely at the heart of most college graduates' perceptions of copyright and intellectual property.

As late as 1996, Lunsford and West could reasonably argue that despite many significant and positive efforts by their colleagues, the bulk of composition pedagogy was perpetuating a narrow and flawed construction of the creator as an owner. Indeed, it is this bias toward understanding writing and creative work as the production of *property* that underpins the *New York Times* editorial. When considering the then-pending *Grokster* case, the *Times* editorial writers could identify no value more compelling than ensuring that "people who create" would retain "the ability to be paid for their work." This bias would also be reflected in the Supreme Court's decision, widely reported as a unanimous rebuke to Grokster, Streamcast, and all purveyors of similar software. When one considers the composition pedagogies that dominated the intellectual landscape when our current Supreme Court justices were educated, this result begins to seem inevitable.

As of this writing, the average age of the Supreme Court Justices is 66. The "average Justice" would have entered college in the late 1950s and graduated during the early 1960s. I cannot fully interrogate the range of possible approaches to teaching writing that the Justices may have encountered. Composition classrooms have historically been contested sites, rife with competing theories and pedagogies. Space precludes a full account of these contests. For my purposes, it will be enough to point to a representative moment from a well-regarded history of U.S. composition instruction that speaks to a baseline understanding that almost certainly colored approaches to composition pedagogy for much of the second half of the twentieth century.

In his *Rhetoric and Reality: Writing Instruction in American Colleges, 1900–1985,* James Berlin cites an article from the first volume of *College Composition and Communication*—published in 1950—by Occidental College Professor Kenneth Oliver. Oliver writes: "[Self-expressive writing] is what has given us the best perspective of man in his process-civilization. Persuasion, inevitably geared down to the masses, can never give us as full a perspective" (qtd. in Berlin109). Berlin glosses this by writing, "Since it is the individual genius who makes for salutary developments in society [. . .] it is the individual genius who should be encouraged in the composition class through literature and expressive writing" (109). The reification of the individual genius, exemplified by Oliver's approach, necessarily reinforces an interpretation of intellectual property law that emphasizes the ownership rights of authors and inventors, and not the public's rights to access, use, and repurpose existing works. Oliver's article thus offers a telling snapshot of the theoretical approaches to the teaching of writing that dominated the U.S. universities when most of our current Supreme Court justices were educated.

My analysis of the written opinions in the *Grokster* case points up the degree to which the current Justices were influenced by the kind of traditionalist composition pedagogy that Lunsford and West critique. The *Grokster* decision is heavily biased toward encouraging the individual genius by rewarding the middlemen who purchase copyrighted work from geniuses. If the public's supposed rights of access and use are compromised by the encouragement of genius (and the concomitant policing of copyright) then that—the Court argues—is the price we must now pay.

Supreme Court decisions have historically offered the best available index as to where the floating line between use and infringement of others' work has settled at any given moment. For this reason, *MGM v. Grokster* has routinely been described as "the most important copyright case in two decades " or, sometimes, "in a generation." These timelines acknowledge, inferentially, that up until Grokster the most significant copyright case involving technologies of reproduction was certainly the 1984 case of *Sony v. Universal Studios,* colloquially known as "the Betamax case." In the wake of the July 2005 decision, we can now understand *Grokster* as the first major challenge to the principle at the heart of *Betamax,* which is articulated quite directly in Justice John Paul Stevens's *Betamax* opinion:

> The staple article of commerce doctrine must strike a balance between a copyright holder's legitimate demand for effective—not merely symbolic—protection of the statutory monopoly, and the rights of others freely to engage in substantially unrelated areas of commerce. Accordingly, the sale of copying equipment, like the sale of other articles of commerce, does not constitute contributory infringement if the product is widely used for legitimate, unobjectionable purposes. Indeed, *it need merely be capable of substantial noninfringing uses.* (emphasis added)

I am by no means the first to suggest that there is a bit of a lacuna between this excerpt's concluding sentence and its predecessors. Stevens begins this critical portion of the opinion by importing a concept from patent law, the notion of a "staple article of commerce." The idea underlying the staple article of commerce doctrine is that it is possible for courts and for the patent office to weigh and determine whether particular inventions were designed for the core purpose of infringing on an existing patent or not. According to the section 35 of the U.S. Code, if a given invention, or component of an invention is "suitable for substantial noninfringing use" it is a "staple article of commerce."

In *Betamax,* Stevens imported the "staple article" from patent law to copyright, and critics have complained that this does violence to the doctrine. Even so, the above-excerpted sentence seems to move from a strong affirmation of the copyright holder's need for protection, to a suggestion that "wide use" for "legitimate, unobjectionable purposes" might constitute a defense against a charge of infringement, before concluding that the *mere capability* of substantial noninfringing uses can serve as a defense against the charge of infringement. This is a remarkable evolution in the space of three sentences. Stevens's last sentence is routinely cited by those who support maximal access to information and to copying technologies. Its predecessors are cited by those pursuing a more restrictive approach.

Taken together, Stevens' sentences form a sort of Rorshach Test. What Stevens said has since been superseded by what others have seen in his sentences. For two decades, the holding in *Betamax* has largely been understood as articulating a principle of judicial non-interference with technologies that have both legal and potentially illegal applications. While the Court's decision does not directly address the legality of the videotape libraries of premium movies that users of the VCR were demonstrably compiling at the time of the decision, the Court was certain that time-shifting programs was a fair use, and elected, in effect, to overlook the infringing applications of the VCR in order to preserve the clearly fair applications.

The *Betamax* standard is necessary for the ongoing development of computer technologies because copying data is fundamental to the operation of computer technologies. In addition to the various copying and shifting of data that is needed to sustain operating systems, the overwhelming majority of computer interactions with the Internet involve at least ephemeral copies of e-mail messages, websites, and other scraps of information, all of which are ostensibly protected by copyright. It should go without saying that I believe the personal computer to be a staple article of commerce. Indeed, I believe it to be, in effect, the direct successor to the Betamax videotape recorder as the "poster child" for the staple article of commerce doctrine. The networked personal computer infringes copyrights *all the time.* But the overwhelming majority of these infringements are *de minimis* multiplied by *de minimis.* The ephemeral copies that sustain our computers are instrumental in enabling the sort of "wide use for legitimate, unobjectionable purposes" that the Supreme Court determined to protect in the *Betamax* case.

But as late as 2000, the RIAA was publicly arguing against the legality of such "staple" uses as storing music on a computer's hard drive.

In a "Frequently Asked Questions" page that built upon the RIAA's campaign against "home taping," the RIAA first acknowledged that "essentially, all copying onto analog media is generally allowed," in order to set the stage for the following argument:

> WHAT YOU CAN'T COPY
>
> Computers and general-purpose computer peripheral devices are not covered by the Audio Home Recording Act. This means they do not pay royalties and they do not incorporate technology to prevent serial copying. As a result, this also means that copying music onto a computer hard drive is not permitted. It is copyright infringement, and a violation of federal law. This is true whether the source being copied is analog or digital; whether you are copying an entire album or just one song or even part of a song; or whether you are making a compilation of songs from albums you already own. The same holds true for copying music off the Internet. While MP3s may be popular, if the artist and record company have not specifically authorized the music to be freely traded on the Net, then posting MP3s to an Internet site or downloading them to your computer hard drive is copyright infringement.
>
> The bottom line: the only digital copying of music that is allowed is with digital recorders that are covered by and comply with the Audio Home Recording Act.

Of course, most digital recorders could not hope to function without the intermediate step of songs being copied to a computer's hard drive. In 1999, the RIAA attempted to sue an early MP3 player (the Diamond "Rio") out of existence using this forlorn line of argument. Judge Diarmud O'Scannlain of the Ninth Circuit Court of Appeals, thankfully, demonstrated little patience for the RIAA's claims. The RIAA has that judge to thank for the half a billion dollars in revenue generated to date by the iTunes Music Store, to say nothing of the music industry's share of subscription fees generated by licensed music services like Rhapsody and Napster 2.0.

Prior to the Supreme Court's decision, *Grokster* promised to definitively answer whether the principles the Court had established for the analog recording medium of the VCR could be productively ported into digital spaces, or, in the alternative, the restrictive approaches to digital media favored by the content industries would carry the day. *Grokster* arrived at the Supreme Court because the RIAA-affiliated MGM records sued the three leading post-Napster peer-to-peer applications: Grokster, Streamcast (the parent of the Morpheus peer-to-peer client) and Sharman BV (at the time the parent of Kazaa) for contributory infringement due to their enabling of unauthorized peer-to-peer downloads. The Australian-based Sharman/Kazaa was split off from the case because of jurisdiction questions. Judge Stephen V. Wilson, of the Los Angeles-based 9th Circuit Court of Appeals surprised many observers by issuing a summary judgment in favor of Grokster and Streamcast, grounded in what appeared to be a flat application of the *Betamax* standard. Wilson wrote:

> Defendants distribute and support software, the users of which can and do choose to employ it for both lawful and unlawful ends. Grokster and StreamCast are not significantly different from companies that sell home video recorders or copy machines, both of which can be and are used to infringe copyrights. (*MGM v. Grokster*)

It is a testament to how much the copyright landscape has shifted that Wilson's ruling surprised anyone. Inevitably, MGM and its RIAA affiliates appealed, and a broad swath of legal scholars settled in, anticipating a ruling that, like *Betamax*, could offer clear guidelines for the fair and reasonable use of a potentially infringing technology.

Unfortunately, the Supreme Court punted.

The Justices' points of agreement are far more circumscribed than the reported "9–0 ruling" suggests. Specifically, the Justices agreed that the *Grokster* case should head back to the 9th Circuit where, in their estimation, summary judgment was improperly awarded to Grokster and Streamcast, and that the 9th Circuit must now rule on whether Grokster and Streamcast should be held liable for having actively induced copyright infringement. With respect to all other issues, this "unanimous" court is strikingly divided, albeit in neat little groups of three. I'll examine each group in turn.

Conclusion: The Cat Came Back

THE "MAJORITY" OPINION: WRITTEN BY SOUTER, AND JOINED BY THOMAS AND SCALIA

This opinion is resolutely focused on protecting the rights of owners (i.e., the copyright holders for popular music and motion pictures that were circulating over peer-to-peer networks). While Souter pays lip service to the notion of public access, the opinion's core focus is establishing the degree to which Grokster and Streamcast structured their businesses to encourage infringement. According to this opinion, the incursion into the copyright holders' rights must be corrected, even at the expense of significant legal usage of Grokster and Streamcast's networks. To this end, Souter's opinion offers a clear substitute for the generally recognized *Betamax* standard. Where in *Betamax*, the Court ruled in favor of the VCR, arguing that it and similar copying technologies "need merely be capable of substantial non-infringing uses." This opinion revises the *Betamax* standard, presenting it as supporting technologies "capable of substantial lawful use." This distinction is important. Both the shift to "capable" from "merely capable" and the substitution of "lawful uses" for "non-infringing uses" are evidence of Souter, Thomas, and Scalia attempting to raise the bar for companies invoking the *Betamax* defense. Judge Wilson suggested that if 10 percent of the material distributed on a peer-to-peer network was non-infringing, then that network had met the *Betamax* standard. This Grokster triumvirate would look askance at that assertion, arguing that the "substantial lawful use threshold had not been reached. Souter and his colleagues misstate Sony in a concluding paragraph when they write, "Sony dealt with a claim of liability based solely on distributing a product with alternative lawful and unlawful uses, with knowledge that some users would follow the unlawful course." The suggestion here is that for the *Betamax* Court, the expectation was that most of the anticipated uses of the VCR would be lawful (i.e., "time-shifting") and that the Court imagined that only a small minority of the VCR users would engage in arguably illicit behavior (i.e., archiving videotapes of programs as substitutes for commercial releases).

In a critical paragraph, these three judges articulate what may come to be known as the "*Grokster* standard."

> Sony's rule limits imputing culpable intent as a matter of law from the characteristics or uses of a distrib-

uted product. But nothing in Sony requires courts to ignore evidence of intent if there is such evidence, and the case was never meant to foreclose rules of fault-based liability derived from the common law.

In other words, while you can't go after Grokster for the design of its products, and the ease with which the products can be used for infringing activities, you are free to pursue Grokster for knowingly and actively structuring its business around the expectation that its software would be used primarily for traffic in infringing files.

The First Concurring Opinion: Written by Breyer, and Joined by Stevens and O'Connor

While Souter's emphasis falls squarely on the maintenance of copyright holders' rights, this opinion offers a realistic assessment of the degree to which all copyrights are subject to low-level infringements, many of which do not merit the time or attention of the judiciary. Where the Souter opinion casts the rights associated with copyright ownership as near-absolute, Breyer describes these rights as sites of contest and near-constant negotiation. For example, Breyer counters the claim that the *Betamax* Court did not anticipate significant infringing use of VCRs by pointing out that Sony had advertised that Betamax owners could use their machines to build libraries of taped copyrighted programs. According to the standard in the Souter decision, this would arguably constitute active inducement of infringement by Sony, but Breyer clearly believes the *Betamax* case was rightly decided, and that the VCR should remain legal. Breyer also questions where the threshold for "non-infringing use" ought to lie, pointing to the "9% or so of authorized time-shifting uses of the VCR" on which the *Betamax* verdict apparently rested.

Breyer's opinion opens with the statement "I agree with the Court that the distributor of a dual-use technology may be liable for the infringing activities of third parties where he or she actively seeks to advance the infringement," but elsewhere in his decision Breyer suggests that the 9th Circuit did not err in awarding summary judgment in this case. The heart of Breyer's opinion is an elegiac testament to the Betamax standard, which he endorses on four grounds: 1) Sony's rule is clear; 2) Sony's rule is strongly technology protecting; 3) Sony's rule

Conclusion: The Cat Came Back

is forward looking; and 4) Sony's rule is mindful of the limitations facing judges where matters of technology are concerned. The import of Breyer's argument is that while the 9th Circuit may have erred in issuing a summary judgment, the proper outcome of the trial ought to again be an affirmation of the *Betamax* standard.

The Second Concurring opinion: Written by Ginsburg, and Joined by Rehnquist and Kennedy

Ginsburg effectively rewrites the *Betamax* doctrine. No longer is the "capability" of substantial non-infringing use the standard. Now, the actual patterns of usage are, apparently, fair game, at least for this trio. This group's distaste for Grokster and Streamcast is readily apparent in a core paragraph, wherein Ginsburg suggests that she, like Souter et al., favors a significantly higher standard than the *Betamax* case's "mere capability." Ginsburg writes:

> Even if the absolute number of noninfringing files copied using the Grokster and StreamCast software is large, it does not follow that the products are therefore put to substantial noninfringing uses and are thus immune from liability. The number of non-infringing copies may be reflective of, and dwarfed by, the huge total volume of files shared. Further, the District Court and the Court of Appeals did not sharply distinguish between uses of Grokster's and StreamCast's software products (which this case is about) and uses of peer-to-peer technology generally (which this case is not about).

Not only is Ginsburg here proposing a radical revision of the Sony standard, she concludes her opinion by pointedly suggesting that the 9th Circuit got the case 180 degrees wrong:

> If, on remand, the case is not resolved on summary judgment in favor of MGM based on Grokster and StreamCast actively inducing infringement, the Court of Appeals, I would emphasize, should reconsider, on a fuller record, its interpretation of Sony's product distribution holding.

Ginsburg is here strongly suggesting that the initial summary judgment for Grokster and Streamcast should be replaced by a summary judgment for MGM. Ginsburg's bias towards maintaining the rights of copyright owners is even more absolute than Souter's. According to Ginsburg, a "large" number of non-infringing files does *not* equal "substantial non-infringing use." Her argument appears to invert *Betamax,* in that it requires courts to focus primarily on the amount of infringing files, and not on the legal activities facilitated by them.

In summary, the Supreme Court's remand of the *Grokster* case to the 9th Circuit carries with it the following advice to the lower court:

- Summary judgment for Grokster and Streamcast was inappropriate. Rehear on the question of whether Grokster and Streamcast actively induced infringement; OR
- Summary judgment for Grokster and Streamcast was inappropriate because you should hold a trial in order to absolve them according to the Betamax standard; OR
- Summary judgment was appropriate, but not for Grokster and Streamcast. And by the way, that Betamax case got it backwards. Focus on the infringing files, not the non-infringing files.

This is a trainwreck.

The aggregate effect of the Grokster decision is to raise the possibility that an examination of a technology inventor's purported intent will likely determine the case if the invention ultimately proves to have infringing uses. *Grokster* thus represents the culmination of a series of incremental steps in which copyright jurisprudence has moved away from a focus on the tangible effects of infringement and toward assessments of whether the developers of a particular information technology or software system adequately addressed the possibility that their products might be used not only for duplication but also for infringement. Such a standard would have made the initial distribution of the photocopier a legally dubious proposition. The *Grokster* decision threatens, in a very real sense, to stifle innovation in digital media until inventors once again sense that intellectual property law promotes the progress of science and useful arts.

Western Rhetoric traces its roots back to the courts and legislature of Athens in the fifth century BCE. The art of persuasive communication has a long history of helping people address, in productive ways, the social and technological challenges they face as citizens of civil society. But the decision in the *Grokster* case makes all too clear that the rhetorical strategies, the metaphors, the tropes, the habits of argument, that were developed for the management of physical property cannot be comfortably and effectively ported to the virtual environs we sometimes call cyberspace. To the extent that a data file is property, it is property that moves and reproduces like *nothing* in the physical landscape, and *Grokster* demonstrates that even our finest jurists lack the rhetorical and theoretical tools needed to productively address digital technologies and their applications. The radical shifts now underway in the teaching of composition and rhetoric hold promise for a future that achieves a better balance between creators' rights and public access. But it will be many years before students educated in this more balanced approach sit on the federal bench, or even achieve majority status in Congress.

As the preceding chapters make clear, my sense is that the U.S. is currently in the process of fumbling an opportunity to productively engage with the intellectual property questions prompted by the rise of the Internet. The past decade's major legislative amendments to copyright—in particular the Copyright Term Extension Act, the Digital Millennium Copyright Act, the No Electronic Theft Act, and the TEACH Act—collectively constitute a disastrous appropriation of rights, privileges, and opportunities formerly understood to belong to the public at large. At the very moment that the most powerful cultural tool in human history—the networked personal computer—has become both widely available and largely affordable, the U.S. is busily drafting laws that reinforce a copyright model optimized long ago for the circulation of print-based media. Never mind that the increasingly broadband network of linked computers can easily send cultural artifacts hurtling around the globe in the space of a few heartbeats. The networked computer, when paired with the processing power available via peer-to-peer networks, offers almost limitless opportunities for the transmission of and access to data. Or rather, these opportunities *would* be almost limitless, were it not for the increasingly restrictive force of intellectual property laws, especially copyright laws.

In fact, over the course of my decade of scholarship directed at understanding the consequences of the Internet for intellectual property policies, I have becoming increasingly pessimistic about the future of the Internet. While Moore's Law continues to deliver substantially faster, smaller, and more affordable computer chips every eighteen months, and broadband access moves from institutions to homes, and even whole cities, the aggregate effect of recent policy decisions and court rulings has been the cordoning off of more than three-quarters of the information that was produced in the twentieth century.

In our overly protected circumstance, paying the full purchase price for a copyrighted work no longer guarantees consistent, efficient access to that work. As I was completing this project, I realized that I was unable to locate my copy of a book that I've cited repeatedly in these pages, Joseph Menn's *All the Rave*. I searched my departmental office, my home office, the stacks of books in my bedroom and the overflow storage in my basement. The book was nowhere to be found. I considered buying a used copy from Amazon, and discovered that they were quite inexpensive. More than one dealer had settled on $3.30 as an appropriate price for a hardcover described as appearing "new." With postage, I could have had a copy within a week or so for under $10.

But as I considered this purchase, I noted that Amazon's website allowed me to search inside the text of Menn's book. I was able to double-check all of my citations, though the interface was a bit cumbersome. At no cost to me, over and above the fees I pay for high-speed broadband access to the Internet, Amazon was offering me a functional copy of my missing print text. In fact, Amazon's version was more readily functional for my purposes (checking citations) than the lost print text. I could readily search the whole of the text, using keywords. I was struck by the ease with which I located passages that had wandered into my text with incomplete or lost page references. This was immeasurably better than the index in my lost print edition. But Amazon would only allow me to read a few pages in sequence. This, no doubt, was based on their interpretation of the reasonable limits of the fair use exception to copyright law. And this made it hard whenever part of a sought after quote hovered on the other side of Amazon's self-imposed limits.

Then I noticed that a digital edition of the text, using Adobe's eBook Reader software, was available from Amazon for $9.95. Having grown habituated to instant gratification, I pulled out my debit card and purchased my second copy of Menn's book. When I opened up this digital copy, I noticed a striking quote that I had, to that point, neglected to include in this project. I highlighted the quote with the "select" feature in my Adobe Reader software and prepared to paste it into my manuscript. And [. . .] got . . . *nothing.*

Through some combination of determinations by Adobe and Crown Business, the Menn book's publisher, the cut-and-paste feature that is available for many PDF files had been disabled for this one. Why? Copyright. And so, as a researcher, I lost a few hours of time. I stopped researching the rhetoric of the peer-to-peer debates and started researching the levels of permission available to purchasers of Adobe ebooks.

This particular Adobe ebook edition was intentionally programmed to eliminate basic functionality because there is the possibility, indeed—given the topic of the book—the likelihood that cut-and-pasted versions of the book's text would circulate online. There is no technological limitation that prevents Adobe from offering more malleable and functional editions of its ebooks. Indeed, some ebooks circulate with no such limitations. This is not a programming problem. Rather, it a problem embedded in the U.S.'s current approach to intellectual property.

Imagine if, instead of a paper copy of this text, my university library, or better yet, the local public library had a copy of the ebook and would lend it to patrons via the Internet. Imagine further that the copy allowed not for wholesale cutting and pasting, but *limited* cutting and pasting—for the sake of argument, we'll use the 10 percent "fair use rule of thumb" that was considered but ultimately rejected by the groups contributing to the 1976 revision of copyright. In a nod to publishers' existing business models, the library would guarantee that only one patron could "check out" the copy at any given time. Many libraries already have "digital reserve" programs that accomplish this sort of restriction. In exchange for this access, library patrons would agree to make available a small amount of bandwidth and processing power, for use in sustaining a peer-to-peer network managed by the libraries in a given state or region. Excess processing power could be sold by the libraries and the revenue could be used to reinforce their collections and sustain the peer-to-peer network.

Everyone would be better off.

Researchers would spend less time tediously retyping the quotations they need to situate their own research. In the event of a recall notice from one patron who urgently needed the text, the timeline for the return of the digital edition would likely be dramatically compressed relative to the timelines for the return of physical texts. Indeed, patrons could arrange novel and expeditious sharing agreements. A night-owl researcher could have the book from sundown to sun-up, while her lark counterpart could access the work as soon as the cock crowed.

Imagine further that the significant bandwidth costs of moving all of these digital materials were predominantly borne not by the libraries (most of which appear to have enough demands on their limited resources) but by the patrons, who would offer spare processing cycles as part of their membership and participation in the library's digital lending program. Perhaps the greatest flaw in the existing frameworks for the delivery of digital materials is the failure to properly take advantage of latent computer power that is now being squandered. The G4 Power Macintosh computer, introduced the same year Shawn Fanning released Napster, was so powerful that the U.S. government initially classified the machines as munitions, and restricted their export to countries perceived as posing a potential risk to the U.S. Most people are using only a small fraction of the processing power within their computer, and wouldn't miss their spare cycles if they were being used elsewhere.

In early 2006, the best estimates were that 70 percent of U.S. active Internet users had access to broadband connections in their homes or workplaces. Broadband connections are conventionally described as "always on." Indeed, part of the appeal of broadband is its ready availability. Users gain almost instant access to the Internet without the shriek of a modem or its attendant delay because ISPs are now habitually offering constantly available bandwidth—bandwidth that in most homes goes unused for at least a *portion* of most nights, or some afternoons, or the occasional morning. We could pool these resources and move mountains of data.

But this won't happen. Indeed, it can't, given the structures currently in place. Technology currently exits that would likely halve the time required to produce research-based writing. But still researchers wade through a swamp of proprietary databases, often unable to remember which of their discipline's journals are available electronically and which are not. Libraries make agonizing decisions about whether to stock particular publications. In the wake of budget cuts, most university libraries have had to make cuts that they rued. This loss of access to research materials is unfolding while the *existing* network of high-speed computers with broadband connections to the Internet—if combined with a streamlined peer-to-peer application and workable guidelines for the preparation of manuscripts—could deliver the whole of recent scholarly research with astonishing efficiency.

The case for peer-to-peer distribution of copyrighted materials does not begin and end with access to last year's big Sheryl Crow hit, or even the complete works of Metallica. The case for peer-to-peer distribution of copyrighted works also involves cultural artifacts like Jeanne Fahnestock's germinal article on the rhetorical shifts in scientific discourse as it moves from disciplinary journals to the popular press, entitled "Accommodating Science." A colleague recently forwarded me a PDF copy of this article that she had, apparently, located while surfing the Internet. I immediately attempted to locate the Internet source for the PDF, and Google was, for once, of no assistance. I know not from whence it came (but there *is* a copyright notice on the first page).

I assign Fahnestock's article regularly in my science writing course. Circulating multiple copies of an article for classroom use is specifically endorsed in the statutory language describing fair use. Most of my students would prefer an electronic copy to a photocopied handout. But am I free to redistribute this e-copy of uncertain provenance? A strict reading of the copyright notice appended to the PDF suggests that I am not. That said, all of my students and I would be allowed to download PDFs of this article were we able to successfully navigate our way through the specific database that houses the archives for *Written Communication* within our university's library system.

But this involves a process that sometimes hinges on psychically divining which of the various electronic databases archives *Written Communication,* or worse, staring blankly at a screen demanding the year, volume, issue, and start page for the article, but *not* allowing me use obvious and distinctive search terms like, say, "Fahnestock" or "Accommodating Science."

Now imagine, for a moment, that the process of locating an academic article or research study was as simple as navigating Napster 1.0 used to be. Participants in this research-based peer-to-peer network—let's call it "Edster" would commit to storing and making available at least ten articles they considered especially helpful. On Edster, you would type in a few key search terms in order to determine whether the article you needed existed in electronic form on the computers of all of the students and colleagues at your university, your region, and/

or throughout your discipline. Imagine receiving a PDF of that article in under a minute *without* navigating through a series of databases, without even firing up the library's proprietary search engine. Imagine how much more efficiently researchers, students, and scholars of all stripes could pursue their research.

But "Edster" can't happen for two reasons. The first is that academic texts, by and large, are subject to the same copyright regime that was developed to protect works like Sheryl Crow's most recent hit single. The second reason is that advocates for broader and fairer use of peer-to-peer technologies have yet to produce an argument as superficially compelling as "stealing music hurts artists." The content industries are winning this debate in large part by drawing upon established tropes that portray college campuses as enclaves of lawlessness and unethical behavior. And when the image most people have of peer-to-peer technologies is yoked to Shawn Fanning's perpetuation of his hacker/undergraduate persona well past its expiration date, the task of rewriting and redirecting the peer-to-peer debate grows incrementally more difficult.

I do not call or wish for the end of copyright. Rather, I seek copyrights calibrated *not* to print delivered by ponies, but to the torrents of information now spanning the globe via broadband peer-to-peer networks.

The consequences of a failure to revise the current peer-to-peer narrative are, ultimately, the abandonment of the principles that prompted the first Congress to title the first U.S. Copyright law, "An Act for the Encouragement of Learning." At this moment, there is no technical hurdle that precludes the distribution of the whole of the Library of Congress' holdings via the Internet. The peer-to-peer protocols that would be required were invented in the last millennium. The bandwidth is available. The scanning will take some time . . . probably years, but the copyright questions (which are, if course, ultimately questions of compensation) are far and away the most challenging aspect of putting scholarly and artistic work online.

In late 2004, the Internet megagiant Google announced, with great fanfare, its plan to digitize the library holdings of five major universities. Google intended to display small portions of the books, limiting users to reviewing a page at a time, and blocking printing. Less than a year later some members of the American Association of University Presses were petitioning the courts, demanding the right to opt out

Conclusion: The Cat Came Back

of having their authors' books scanned. Other publishers are now demanding that Google request and receive permissions for each book it scans. And, for good measure, free speech advocates are encouraging Google to refuse to honor the publishers' wishes and publish everything based on a hard-line fair use claim. Once again, U.S. Copyright Law has magically transformed an attempt to build Borges's Library of Babel into the Tower of Babel, wherein the participants are unable to communicate with one another, and progress toward lofty goals is impossible.

That said, peer-to-peer technologies have been reaching for the heavens for some time, and doing so with a remarkable coordination and efficiency. According to recent estimates, over five million users of the SETI@home peer-to-peer network have donated nineteen *billion* cycles of processing power to searching the heavens for signs of intelligent extraterrestrial life. To put this in a *kind* of perspective, a single computer would need to work well over two *million* years to process the data that the collective network of computers has processed since 1999. And even this is a false comparison, as SETI@Home depends, in significant part, on the presence of an array of networked computers for its functionality. But to date, this massive investment of computer power has delivered only silence. The SETI project is visionary and exciting, and well removed from the kinds of copyright squabbles and concerns that have hamstrung other peer-to-peer endeavors.

Back here on earth, in the U.S., our national keeper of the putatively public notices of copyright registration and renewal—the information needed to determine whether a given work is protected by copyright or public domain—is the Library of Congress. Those wishing to determine whether a particular work was renewed can search in vain on the Library of Congress's website, until they eventually arrive at this notice:

> Can you tell me who owns a copyright?
>
> We can provide you with the information available in our records. A search of registrations, renewals, and recorded transfers of ownership made before 1978 requires a manual search of our files. Upon request, our staff will search our records at the statutory rate of $150 for each hour. There is no fee if you conduct

a search in person at the Copyright Office. (U.S. Copyright Office)

With a measure of initiative, and a collective commitment to an ethical and equitable rebalancing of our nation's copyright laws, the rich storehouses of information within this, the world's second largest library, could be available not only to those who have $150 an hour to spare, not only to those who have the opportunity to search at the Library in person, but to *anyone* with a networked computer. We could assure the bandwidth and processing power needed for this project if we required each visitor to—however briefly—repurpose his or her computer as a "peer," helping to catalog and circulate the Library's staggering collection. We might even leverage this processing power to generate revenue, and thereby compensate copyright holders. We have the technologies required. The only question is whether we have the *will* to constructively challenge and revise the laws that now make this idea impossible.

To date, the most successful implementation of peer-to-peer technologies is dedicated to marking off quadrants of space where there are, so far, no traces of intelligent extraterrestrial life. Surely, with SETI's success as a model, a few million people could be persuaded to contribute their spare cycles and excess bandwidth to the peer-to-peer enabled project of searching the libraries of earth for the traces of intelligent terrestrial life.

Appendix: On Images and Permissions

Earlier in this text, I write, following Rebecca Moore Howard, that "contemporary scholarship absolutely depends on building on others' work. There are many circumstances when a requirement to secure permission would be recognized as unnecessary, or would result in de facto censorship." These words echoed in my mind as I weighed how to respond to my publisher's request for permission information for some of the images reproduced in this book. In reviewing my use of others' materials within this text, I have arrived at the conclusion that all of my uses fall well within the orbit of fair use, as outlined in the U.S. Copyright Code. While I have done my best to identify and acknowledge the copyright holders for these images, I have determined not to seek permissions for these obviously fair uses. Further, I believe it would be outrageous if, through overt denial of a permissions request or even tardy response, an organization like, say, the MPAA could foreclose my reproduction and critical assessment of a screenshot from a website the MPAA had made generally available throughout the Internet. Such a result would, in my estimation, be a suppression of critical speech in violation of the First Amendment. It would also be an absurd result if contemporary U.S. copyright law, descended from a 1790 law entitled "An Act for the Encouragement of Learning . . ." were to be mobilized to strip a text like this of its few, necessary illustrations.

My University of Minnesota colleague, Laura Gurak, arrived at a similar conclusion as she reviewed her use of others' materials within her 2001 book, *Cyberliteracy: Navigating the Internet with Awareness*, published by Yale University Press. Gurak describes her use of materials as meeting the conventional standards for fair use:

> My use of the material in this book, along with its purpose for scholarly criticism, is educational, based on previously published material, uses only the amount needed to make the point, and does not have any negative impact on the value of the original. (If anything, the examples used in this book bring positive value to the original by pointing readers to these sources.)
>
> I thus have made the choice to obtain written permission only on items that were more of an embellishment to my narrative than an item used for overt criticism. Also, I have not obtained permission to use Web pages. For one, the Web pages used herein are used for criticism. In addition, when a person or organization makes a Web site available to the world, that person or organization knows full well that the resulting Web page will be uploaded onto thousands of computer screens, linked to by other Web sites, and printed out on desktop laser printers. None of these uses requires written permission, and a book, especially an act of criticism, is hardly different. (162)

In the half-decade since Gurak wrote these words, little has changed. While the Internet is a core tool for most twenty-first century researchers, most of us still face uncertainty with respect to fundamental questions of scholarly use and access. But this much seems clear. When a researcher takes a screenshot of a Web page and then analyzes and critiques it, this must not be understood as either infringement or theft. Rather, this activity is the very essence of what our laws have protected for more than two centuries.

We must not surrender this tradition to a process that would, functionally, allow the targets of criticism to hamper or dilute that criticism based on a specious or arbitrary denial of permission to reproduce the object under discussion.

It is conventional for Web-based composers to clip and critique material found elsewhere on the Web. Indeed, the relatively new and exciting genre of blogs (or, more formally, Web Logs) would be crippled by a projection of the print permissions culture into cyberspace. This book makes modest, and fair use of materials found on the Internet.

Were it a website, these uses would be unremarkable. Even within this book they are not especially remarkable. What is remarkable, however, is that we as a culture remain uncertain as to whether a composer in my position needs to ask permission before critiquing, or not. My fond wish, as the preceding pages make clear, is that books like this one help move us toward a culture that more thoughtfully and knowledgably examines the practical, ethical, and legal consequences of digital media.

Works Cited

Abelson, Hal, et al. "Brief Amici Curiae of Computer Science Professors." *Electronic Frontier Foundation*. 2005. EFF.org. 22 May 2006 <http://www.eff.org/IP/P2P/MGM_v_Grokster/20050301_cs_profs.pdf>.

Adar, Eytan, and Bernardo Huberman. "Free Riding on Gnutella." *First Monday* 2000. FirstMonday.com. 20 Aug. 2006 <http://www.firstmonday.org/issues/issue5_10/adar/index.html>.

Albini, Steve. "The Problem With Music." *Negativland.com*. 1993. 20 Aug. 2006 <http://www.negativland.com/albini.html>.

Alderman, John. "Free for all." *The Guardian* 4 Aug. 2001, sec. Guardian Weekend: 50. LexisNexis. 13 Aug. 2005.

—. *Sonic Boom: Napster, MP3, and the New Pioneers of Music*. Cambridge, MA: Perseus, 2001.

Archerd, Army. "Pirated DVDs in an Alley Near You." *Variety* 11 Aug. 2003. Variety.com. 20 Apr. 2005.

Barry, Hank. "Testimony of Hank Barry, Chief Executive Officer, Napster, Inc., Before the Senate Judiciary Committee." 11 July 2000. Senate.gov. 20 Aug. 2006 <http://judiciary.senate.gov/oldsite/7112000_hb.htm>.

Basic Books, Inc. v. Kinko's Graphics Corporation. Ed. 758 F. Supp. 1522. Vol. 89 CIV. 2807 (CBM). S.D.N.Y., 1991.

Berlin, James A. *Rhetoric and Reality: Writing Instruction in American Colleges, 1900–1985*. Carbondale, IL: Southern Illinois UP, 1987.

Black, Edwin. *Rhetorical Criticism : A Study in Method*. Madison: U of Wisconsin P, 1978.

Boehlert, Eric. "MP3.Com Sues RIAA Right Back." *RollingStone.com News*. 2000. WholeNote.com. 20 Apr. 2005 <http://www.wholenote.com/default.asp?iTarget=http%3A//www.wholenote.com/news/item.asp%3Fi%3D132>.

Boliek, Brooks. "Mouse Grouse: Dis Boss Lays into Computer Biz." *The Hollywood Reporter*. 2002. TheHollywoodReporter.com. 20 Apr. 2005 <http://www.larta.org/pl/NewsArticles/02Marc01_HR_Eisner.htm>.

Borland, John. "Metallica, Dr. Dre Urge Colleges to Cut Napster Access." *C/NET*. 8 Sep. 2000. C/NET News.com. 20 Apr. 2005 <http://news.com.com/2100-1023-245505.html>.

Bronfman, Edgar. "Keynote Address: Aspen Summit, Building a Digital Ownership Society: The Place for Property and Commons." 22 Aug. 2005. 24 Aug. 2005 <http://www.tvworldwide.com/events/pff/050821/agenda.htm>.

Burk, Dan L. "Jurisdiction in a World without Borders." *Virginia Journal of Law and Technology* 1.3 Spring 1997. 20 Aug. 2006 <http://scs.student.virginia.edu/~vjolt/text_only/vol1/home_art3.html>.

Burke, Kenneth. *A Rhetoric of Motives.* Berkeley: 1950. U of California P, 1969.

Carroll, Terry. "Frequently Asked Questions About Copyright (v. 1.1.2)." 17 Dec. 1993. *Uni-Giessen.de* 20 Apr. 2005 <http://www.uni-giessen.de/faq/archiv/copyright-faq.part1-6/msg00002.html>.

Chmielewski, Dawn. "Online Film Piracy Cuts into Industry Profit." *San Jose Mercury News.* 30 May 2002. BayArea.com. 20 Apr. 2005 <http://www.bayarea.com/mld/bayarea/business/technology/3369706.htm>.

Coyle, Michael, and Jon Dolan. "Modeling Authenticity, Authenticating Commercial Models." *Reading Rock and Roll: Authenticity, Appropriation, Aesthetics.* Ed. Kevin J. H. Dettmar and William Richey. New York: Columbia UP, 1999. 17–35.

Crowley, Sharon, and Debra Hawhee. *Ancient Rhetorics for Contemporary Students.* Boston: Allyn and Bacon, 1999.

Dansby, Andrew. "Dr. Dre Takes Napster to Court." *RollingStone.com News* 27 Apr. 2000. FortuneCity.de 20 Aug. 2006. <http://www.fortunecity.de/kraftwerk/goldi/326/Magazines/RollingStone_000427/index.html#>

Davis, Janet. "Stasis Theory." *Encyclopedia of Rhetoric and Composition.* Ed. Theresa Enos. New York: Garland, 1996. 693–695.

Evangelista, Benny. "Will Napster Get Nailed? Firm's Peace Overtures Ignored by Recording Industry." *San Francisco Chronicle* 2 Oct. 2000, sec. Business: D1. LexisNexis. 15 Aug. 2005.

Fahnestock, Jeanne R., and Marie J. Secor. "Grounds for Argument: Stasis Theory and the Topoi." *Argument in Transition: Proceedings of the Third Summer Conference on Argumentation.* Ed. David Zarefsky, Malcolm O. Sillars, and Jack Rhodes. Annandale, VA: Speech Communication Association, 1983. 135–146.

Fahnestock, Jeanne R. "Accommodating Science: The Rhetorical Life of Scientific Facts." *Written Communication* 3.3 (1986): 275–96.

Feist Publications, Inc. v. Rural Telephone Service Co. Vol. 499 U.S. 340, 1991.

Fitzpatrick, Eileen. "Napster Ruling may Affect Other Sites." *Billboard* 5 Aug. 2000: 5+.

Foucault, Michel. *The Archaeology of Knowledge.* New York: Pantheon Books, 1972.

"Free Compact Discs More Headache than Blessing for Libraries." *USA Today.* 2 Aug. 2004, sec. Tech.

Gold, Robert. "'U' Concerned about MP3 use." *The Michigan Daily* 2 Feb 2000, sec. 1: 1.

Goldstein, Paul. *Copyright's Highway : From Gutenberg to the Celestial Jukebox.* New York: Hill and Wang, 1994.

Gonzalez, David. "At Cuba Conference, Old Foes Exchange Notes on 1962 Missile Crisis." *New York Times* 14 Oct. 2002, Late Edition ed., sec. A: 6+.

Greenfeld, Karl Taro. "The Free Juke Box." *Time* 27 Mar. 2000, 82.

—. "Meet the Napster." *Time* 25 Sep. 2000. 60-7.

Grover, Ron. "Box-Office Boom, Profit Gloom." *Business Week Online.* 2002. 20 Aug. 2006 <http://www.businessweek.com/bwdaily/dnflash/jun2002/nf20020614_7543.htm>.

Gurak, Laura J. *Cyberliteracy: Navigating the Internet with Awareness.* New Haven: Yale UP, 2001.

Hakluyt, Richard. "The True Pictures and Fashions of the People in That Parte of America Now Called Virginia, Discovured by Englishmen." 1590. *Rootsweb.com.* 20 Aug. 2006 <http://freepages.genealogy.rootsweb.com/~vagirl/Lineage_Quest_Library/Historical_Accounts/true_pictures_and_fashions.htm>.

—. "Voyages in Search of The North-West Passage." *University of Adelaide Library Electronic Texts Collection.* Ed. Steve Thomas. 1577. 20 Aug. 2006 <http://etext.library.adelaide.edu.au/h/hakluyt/northwest/chapter4.html>.

Hansen, Evan, and Lisa M. Bowman. "Court: Napster Filters must be Foolproof." C/NET. 12 July 2001. C/NET News.com. 20 Apr. 2005 <http://news.com.com/Court+Napster+filters+must+be+foolproof/2100-1023_3-269837.html>.

Harmon, Amy. "Black Hawk Download: Pirated Videos Thrive Online." *New York Times.* 17 Jan. 2002. Nytimes.com. 20 Apr. 2005 <http://www.nytimes.com/2002/01/17/technology/circuits/17VIDE.htm>.

Harper, Georgia, and the University of Texas System Crash Course in Copyright. "The TEACH Act Finally Becomes Law." *University of Texas System Crash Course in Copyright.* 13 Nov. 2002. 20 Apr. 2005.

Hayden, Tom, et al. "Port Huron Statement." 1962. 20 Aug. 2006 <http://lists.village.virginia.edu/sixties/HTML_docs/Resources/Primary/Manifestos/SDS_Port_Huron.html>.

Himanen, Pekka. *The Hacker Ethic, and the Spirit of the Information Age.* New York: Random House, 2001.

King, Brad. "He Wants His My.mp3.Com." *WIRED* 15 Mar 2000. Wired.com. 20 Apr. 2005 <http://www.wired.com/news/business/0,1367,34816-2,00.html?tw=wn_story_page_next1>.

Konrad, Rachel. "Makers of MP3 Players Distance Themselves from Napster." C/NET. 12 Feb. 2001. C/NET News.com. 20 Apr. 2005 <http://news.com.com/2100-1023-252478.html?legacy=cnet>.

—. "Napster Fans Frantically Download Tunes." 28 July 2000. C/NET News.com. 20 Apr. 2005 <http://news.com.com/2100-1023-243816.html?legacy=cnet>.

Kornblum, Janet. "Napster Close to Deal with Recording Giants." *USA Today* Tech 5 June 2001. Usatoday.com 20 Apr. 2005 <http://www.usatoday.com/tech/news/2001-06-05-ebrief.htm>.

Leeds, Jeff. "Apple, Digital Music's Angel, Earns Record Industry's Scorn." *New York Times.* 27 Aug. 2005. A1.

Lefevre, Karen Burke. *Invention as a Social Act.* Carbondale, IL: Southern Illinois UP, 1986.

Leff, Michael. "Hermeneutical Rhetoric." *Rhetoric and Hermeneutics in Our Time: A Reader.* Ed. Michael J.. Hyde and Walter Jost. New Haven: Yale UP, 1997. 196-214.

Lessig, Lawrence. *Free Culture: How Big Media Uses Technology and the Law to Lock Down Culture and Control Creativity.* New York: Penguin Press, 2004.

—. *The Future of Ideas: The Fate of the Commons in a Connected World.* New York: Random House, 2001.

Levy, Steven. *Hackers: Heroes of the Computer Revolution.* Rev. ed. New York: Penguin Books, 1994.

—. *Hackers: Heroes of the Computer Revolution.* Garden City, NY: Anchor Press/Doubleday, 1984.

Lichstein, Henry. "Telephone Hackers Active." *The Tech* 43.83 20 Nov. 1963. 20 Aug. 2006 <http://www-tech.mit.edu.floyd.lib.umn.edu/archives/VOL_083/TECH_V083_S0315_P001.pdf>.

Litman, Jessica. "War and Peace: The 34th Annual Donald C. Brace Lecture." *Journal of the Copyright Society of the USA* 53 (2005): 1. 20 Aug. 2006. < http://www-personal.umich.edu/%7Ejdlitman/papers/34thBraceLecture.pdf >.

—. "War Stories." *Cardozo Arts & Entertainment Law Journal* 20 (2002): 337.

—. *Digital Copyright : Protecting Intellectual Property on the Internet.* Amherst, N.Y.: Prometheus Books, 2001.

Love, Courtney. "Courtney Love Does the Math." *Salon.com.* 14 June 2000. 20 Aug. 2006 < http://archive.salon.com/tech/feature/2000/06/14/love/>

Lunsford, Andrea A., and Susan West. "Intellectual Property and Composition Studies." *College Composition and Communication* 47.3 (1996): 383–411.

Macavinta, Courtney. "RIAA Sues MP3.Com, Alleges Copyright Violations." *C/NET.* 21 Jan. 2000. C/NET News.com. 20 Apr. 2005 <http://news.com.com/2100-1023-235953.html>.

Mailloux, Steven. "Rhetorical Hermeneutics Revisited." *Text and Performance Quarterly* 11 (1991): 233–48.

—. *Rhetorical Power.* Ithaca, NY: Cornell UP, 1989.

Mainelli, Tom. "Apple Unveils Online Music Service." *PC World.* 28 Apr. 2003. Pcworld.com. 20 Aug. 2006 <http://pcworld.about.com/news/Apr282003id110482.htm>.

McLuhan, Marshall, and Quentin Fiore. *The Medium Is the Massage.* New York: Bantam Books, 1967.

Mehr, Bob. "Gnat, Meet Cannon." *The Chicago Reader* 2 May 2004. Chicagoreader.com. 20 Aug. 2006 <http://www.chicagoreader.com/TheMeter/050204.html>.

Menn, Joseph. *All the Rave: The Rise and Fall of Shawn Fanning's Napster.* New York: Crown Business, 2003.

Merriden, Trevor. *Irresistible Forces: The Business Legacy of Napster & the Growth of the Underground Internet.* Oxford: Capstone, 2001.

Metro Goldwyn-Mayer Studios, Inc. v. Grokster, Ltd. Ed. 259 F. Supp. 2d 1029, 2003.

MGM Studios, Inc., v. Grokster, Ltd. Ed. 545 U. S. , 125 S. Ct. 2764. Vol. (04–0480), 2005.

Mitten, Christopher. *Shawn Fanning: Napster and the Music Revolution.* Brookfield, CT: Twenty-First Century Books, 2002.

Motion Picture Association of America. "Illegal Downloading: Inappropriate for All Ages." *mpaa.org.* 25 Aug. 2005. 20 Aug. 2006 <http://www.mpaa.org/press_releases/2005_08_25.pdf>.

Oberholzer, Felix, and Koleman Strumpf. "The Effect of File Sharing on Record Sales: An Empirical Analysis." Mar. 2004. 20 Aug. 2006. <http://www.unc.edu/~cigar/papers/FileSharing_March2004.pdf>.

Patterson, Lyman Ray. *Copyright in Historical Perspective.* Nashville, TN: Vanderbilt UP, 1968.

Porter, James E. "Intertextuality and the Discourse Community." *Rhetoric Review* 5.1 (1986): 34–47.

Rader. "Re: Look, this is silly." *Slashdot.* 26 Feb. 2000. slashdot.org. 20 Aug. 2006 <http://slashdot.org/comments.pl?sid=10781&cid=401120>.

Recording Industry Association of America. "725 Additional Illegal File Sharers Cited In New Wave of Copyright Infringement Lawsuits." *RIAA.* 27 Apr. 2005. riaa.com. 20 Aug. 2006 <http://www.riaa.com/News/newsletter/042705.asp>.

—. "Recording Industry to Begin Collecting Evidence and Preparing Lawsuits Against File 'Sharers' Who Illegally Offer Music Online." *RIAA.* 25

June 2003. riaa.com. 20 Aug. 2006 <http://www.riaa.com/News/newsletter/062503.asp>.

Rosen, Hilary. "RIAA Statement Concerning MP3.Com's Counter Lawsuit." *RIAA*. 8 Feb. 2000. riaa.com. 20 Aug. 2006 <http://www.riaa.com/news/newsletter/press2000/020800.asp>.

Ross, Andrew. "Hacking Away at the Counterculture." *Postmodern Culture* 1.1 (1990): 1–43. 20 Aug. 2006 <http://www.infomotions.com/serials/pmc/pmc-v1n1-ross-hacking.txt>.

Rothstein, Edward. "Swashbuckling Anarchists Try to Eliminate Copyrights from Cyberspace." *New York Times*. 10 June 2000. Nytimes.com. 20 Aug. 2006 <http://www.nytimes.com/library/tech/00/06/biztech/articles/10copyright.htm>.

Rozhon, Tracie, and Rachel Thorner. "They Sell No Fake before Its Time; on the Streets, Genuine Copies (and a Few Originals)." *New York Times* 26 May 2005, sec. Business/Financial: C5.27 May 2005.

Ruling in MP3.Com—Unofficial Version., 6 Sep. 2000. Nysd.uscourts.gov. 20 Apr. 2005 <http://www.nysd.uscourts.gov/courtweb/pdf/D02NYSC/00-09078.pdf>.

Segaller, Stephen. *Nerds 2.0.1: A Brief History of the Internet.* New York: TV Books, 1998.

Sony Corp. of Amer. v. Universal City Studios, Inc. Vol. 464 U.S. 417, 1984.

Stallman, Richard M. (Cambridge Mass.). *Free Software, Free Society : Selected Essays of Richard M. Stallman.* Ed. Joshua Gay. Boston, MA: Free Software Foundation, 2002.

Stapp, Scott. "What Artists & Songwriters Say." *MusicUnited.* 6 Nov. 2002. MusicUnited.org. 20 Aug. 2006 <http://www.musicunited.org/3_artists.html>.

Strauss, Neil. "File-Sharing Battle Leaves Musicians Caught in the Middle." *New York Times* 14 Sep. 2003. 1:1.

Sullivan, Lorraine. "Statement of Lorriane Sullivan, Senate Committee on Governmental Affairs." 30 Sep. 2003. senate.gov. 20 Aug. 2006 <http://www.senate.gov/~govt-aff/index.cfm?Fuseaction=Hearings.Testimony&HearingID=120&WitnessID=421>.

Suplee, Curt, and Evelyn Richards. "Computers Vulnerable, Panel Warns; Networks Susceptible to Hackers, Accidents." *Washington Post* 6 Dec. 1990, Final ed., sec. First Section: A1.

Thomas, Douglas. *Hacker Culture.* Minneapolis: U of Minnesota P, 2002.

U.S. Copyright Office. "Services of the Copyright Office (FAQ)." *U.S. Copyright Office.* 20 Aug. 2006 <http://www.copyright.gov/help/faq/faq-services.html>.

Ulrich, Lars. "Statement of Lars Ulrich Before the Committee on the Judiciary United States Senate." *RIAA.* 11 July 2000. RIAA.com. 20 Aug. 2006 <http://www.riaa.com/News/newsletter/press2000/071100.asp>.

UMG Recordings, Inc. v. MP3.Com, Inc., 92 F. Supp. 2nd 349. 2000.

Vaidhyanathan, Siva. *The Anarchist in the Library: How the Clash between Freedom and Control is Leaving Cyberspace and Entering the Real World.* New York: Basic Books, 2004.

—. "Copyright as Cudgel." *Chronicle of Higher Education* 2 Aug. 2002. Chronicle.com. 20 Aug. 2006 <http://chronicle.com/free/v48/i47/47b00701.htm>.

—. *Copyrights and Copywrongs : The Rise of Intellectual Property and how it Threatens Creativity.* New York: New York UP, 2001.

Varanini, Giancarlo. "Q&A: Napster Creator Shawn Fanning." 2 Mar. 2000. ZDNet. 15 Aug. 2005 <http://news.zdnet.com/2100–9595_22–502047.html?legacy=zdnn>.

Wah. "Re: Look, this is silly." *Slashdot.* 26 Feb. 2000. slashdot.org. 20 Aug. 2006 <http://slashdot.org/comments.pl?sid=10781&cid=401279>.

"When David Steals Goliath's Music." *New York Times.* 28 Mar. 2005. Nytimes.com. 20 Aug. 2006 <http://select.nytimes.com/search/restricted/article?res=F30914FB3E5B0C7B8EDDAA0894DD404482>.

Wu, Tim. "Exit Valenti." *Lessig Blog.* 2 Aug. 2004. 20 Aug. 2006 <http://www.lessig.org/blog/archives/002065.shtml>.

Yoos, George. "Ethos." *Encyclopedia of Rhetoric and Composition.* Ed. Theresa Enos. New York: Garland, 1996. 410–14.

Zikzak. "Re: Look, this is silly." *Slashdot.* 26 Feb. 2000. slashdot.org. 20 Apr. 2005 <http://slashdot.org/comments.pl?sid=10781&cid=401213>.

Index

AAUP (American Association of University Presses), 146
Abelson, Hal, 128
Adar, Eytan, 99
Adobe eBook Reader, 142–43
Albini, Steve: "The Problem with Music," 118
Alpert, Herb, and the Tijuana Brass, 3–4
Altnet, 119
Amazon.com, 18, 59, 72, 142
American Revolution, 110
anaphora, 108
Apple Computer, Inc., 61–6; iTunes Music Store, 65, 86, 122–23, 135
Archerd, Army, 73–74
Aristotle, 7, 38; *arête*, 39; *eunoia*, 39; *phronesis*, 39
Army of Mice (parody of the MPAA), 123–25
ARPANET, 128
Athens, 140
Audio Home Recording Act of 1991, 57–58, 89, 95, 135
authorship, 130–32

bandwidth, 13, 98, 143–44, 146, 148
Barry, Hank, 34, 106, 109–10
Basic Books v. Kinko's, 16
Beastie Boys, 102–3
Bennett, Jay, 103
Berlin Wall, 115

Berlin, James: *Rhetoric and Reality*, 132
Berne Convention, 74–75
"Betamax Case," *See Universal Studios v. Sony*
Billboard, 102
BitTorrent, 6, 123
Black, Edwin, 20
Blackmun, Harry, 56
Blockbuster, 106
BMG Music et al. v. Gonzalez, 91–92. 97
Bond, James, 119
Borges, Jorge Luis: "The Library of Babel," 19, 147
Bowie, David, 77
Brewster, Sir David, 69
Breyer, Stephen, 138
broadband, 14, 86, 99, 105–6, 141–42, 144–46
Bronfman, Edgar, 108–9, 122–23
Burk, Dan, 20, 120
Burke, Kenneth: identification, 40–41

C/NET, 56, 65
Cake (band), 86–87
cassette tape, 28–29, 63–64, 91, 117
Chaucer, Geoffrey, 70
Chicago Reader, 91
Churchill, Winston, 108
client-server, 128
Cold War, 25, 106–7, 112–19, 126

College Composition and Communication, 132
compact discs, 3, 10–13, 53, 59, 61, 63–65, 68, 72, 74–75, 77, 81, 91–95, 102–3, 110, 112, 117–18
composition pedagogy, 131–32
Computers and Composition, 130
content industries, 6, 12, 52, 66, 68, 76–77, 82–83, 105, 108, 116, 121–26, 136, 146
copyright: Napster users' perceptions of, 3–5 U.S. Copyright Act, 4, 5, 15, 51; limitations of Western approach, 8–12; misunderstanding of, 14, 19–20, 88; education and, 15–19; and freedom of expression, 45–46; transformed by digital media 47–48; expansion of control ceded to owners, 48–50, 141; fixity requirement, 52, 108–9; U.S. Supreme Court's emphasis on public benefit, 55–56, 78, 81; Dickens's campaign for international copyright, 74; "life plus" terms ushered in by Berne, 75; Canadian copyright law, 91; computer use as *de facto* infringement, 134–35; "inducement" 140; recalibration of, 146; U.S. Copyright Office, 148. *See also* fair use
counterfeit, counterfeiting, 9, 105; as alternative to "piracy" 68–75
Coyle Michael, 39
crackers, 22–24, 32, 39
Creative Commons, 28, 100–3
CRIA (Canadian Recording Industry Association), 91
Crow, Sheryl, 103, 145–46
Crowley, Sharon, 121
Crown Business (publisher), 143

Cuban Missile Crisis, 115, 118
cyberspace, 29, 87, 120, 141, 150

DAT (Digital Audio Tape), 57
Davie Allan and the Arrows, 59
Davis, Janet, 120
de minimis, 58–60, 89–91, 104, 134
Declaration of Independence, 110
Depp, Johnny, 71
Descartes, Rene, 97
Desk Set, 17–18
détente, 115, 121
Diamond Rio (MP3 player), 135
Dickens, Charles, 20, 74; *Oliver Twist*, 20
digital media, 21, 29, 31–32, 45–47, 52–54, 57–65, 76–77, 85–86, 108–9, 135–36, 140–44, 151
distance education, 16–19
DMCA (Digital Millennium Copyright Act), 19, 113, 141
Dolan, John, 39
Domoshnyaya Kollektsiya, 10–11
Download.com, 12–13
downloading. *See* file transfers
Dr. Dre, 5, 41–43
DRM (digital rights management), 8
DVD (Digital Video Disc), 18, 63, 72–76

Ede, Lisa, 130
Edison, Thomas Alva, 101
EFF (Electronic Frontier Foundation), 100–3
8-track tape cartridges, 117
Eisner, Michael, 61
e-mail, 9, 52, 109, 134
Eminem, 50–51
Eno, Brian, 10
ethos, 7, 26, 37–43

Fahnestock, Jeanne, 120; "Accommodating Science," 145
fair use, 15–16, 47–48, 50–51, 58, 60, 81–82, 89, 104, 134, 142–43, 145–47, 149–50
Fanning, Shawn, 3, 32–44, 67, 109, 144, 146
file shariing. *See* file transfers
file transfers, 14, 21, 44, 58, 68, 88, 100, 102, 104, 105, 107–8, 114, 117, 119, 121
Fiore, Quentin, 2
Flynn, Errol, 71
45 rpm single, 117
Foucault, Michel: archaeological method, 20

George III, 110
Gilbert and Sullivan, 71
Ginsburg, Ruth Bader, 139–40
Gnutella, 6, 86, 99
Goldstein, Paul, 47–48
Goldwater, Barry, 106
Google, 145–46
Grateful Dead, 28–29
Greenblatt, Stephen: new historicism, 21
Greenfeld, Karl Taro, 35, 52
Grokster Case. *See MGM v. Grokster*
Gurak, Laura: *Cyberliteracy* and its treatment of permissions, 149–50

hackers, 9, 12, 21, 22–44, 74, 105, 110–12, 119, 121, 146
Hakluyt, Richard, 70
Hatch, Orrin, 42
Hawhee, Debra, 121
Hawisher, Gail, 130
HBO, 58, 106
Heckler, Steve, 108
Hendrix, Jimi, 55
Hermagoras of Temnos, 120

Hillebrand, Laura, 72. *See also* Seabiscuit
Himanen, Pekka: *The Hacker Ethic*, 23–24
Hollywood, 33, 76, 106
Howard, Rebecca Moore, 20, 83, 149
Huberman, Bernardo, 99

Iglauer, Bruce, 88
intellectual property, 7–8, 14–15, 17, 28, 31, 40, 47–48, 55, 60, 71, 78, 81, 83, 108–9, 120–21, 126, 129–32, 140–43
Internet: dependence on content, 13, use in education and research 14–15, roots in 1960s counterculture 26–29; as site for innovative distribution of music 102; centrality of peer-to-peer technologies, 127–29; latent potential of, 144–46
ISPs (Internet Service Providers), 91, 108, 144
inventors, 20, 38, 48, 75, 78, 132, 140
iPod, 59, 62–65, 91; initial dependence upon Napster 64

Jaszi, Peter, 20
Jefferson, Thomas, 130
Jobs, Steve, 65–66, 123
Johnson, Lyndon, 106
Jolson, Al, 101, 103

Kaempfert, Bert, 3
Kazaa, 6, 12, 13, 90–100, 119, 136; Kazaa Media Desktop, 12, 97–98
Kennedy, Anthony, 139
LeFevre, Karen Burke, 20, 130; *Invention as a Social Act*, 130
Lessig, Lawrence, 20, 28, 102; *Free Culture*, 82–83, 102; *The Future of Ideas*, 85

Levy, Steven, 24–28, 30; articulation of the "Hacker Ethic," 27–28.
Lewis and Clark, 26
LEXIS-NEXIS, 14
libraries, 14–15, 18, 19, 117, 143–48
Library of Congress, 146–47
Limewire, 86, 103, 119
Litman, Jessica, 20, 67–69, 81–82, 88, 114, 126; *Digital Copyright*, 14, 67, 114
LoadPod, 64
logos, 7
LokiTorrent, 123
Love, Courtney, 118
LP (long playing record), 117
Lucas, George, 43
Luckombe, Philip, 69
Lunsford, Andrea, 20, 130–32

Madonna, 40, 119, 124
Madonna Remix Project, 119, 124
Mailloux, Steven: rhetorical hermeneutics, 21–22
Malcom, John, 123
Manson, Marilyn, 9
McLuhan, Marshall, 2
Menn, Joseph: *All the Rave*, 32–36, 40, 44; copy-protected eBook edition of ,142–143
Merriden, Trevor: *Irresistible Forces*, 36, 108
Merry Pranksters, 26
Metallica, 5, 40–43, 53, 55, 104, 116, 145
MGM v. Grokster, 128–41
MIT (Massachusetts Institute of Technology), 23
Morpheus, 136
MP3, 4, 9, 10–13, 40, 56, 59, 62–65, 80, 82, 85– 88, 91, 94–96, 102–4, 109, 111, 113, 119, 135

MP3.com: my.mp3.com, 59, 77–82; Beam-It, 77, 79
MPAA (Motion Picture Association of America), 6, 82, 105–6, 123, 125, 149
MTV (Music TeleVision), 41, 43

Napster: popularity of, 3–6; roots in hacker community 32–44; iconography 35, 127; associated with theft, 52– 56, and *Betamax* standard 58; efficiencies of 59; ties to rock and hip-hop 63–64; positioned as enabling piracy, 67–68; 77–82, community building features of 96; as revolutionary 109–10
Napster 2.0, 122, 127, 135
NASA (National Aeronautics and Space Administration), 25–26
NET (No Electronic Theft) Act of 1997, 49, 52, 141
New York Times, 44, 74, 86, 105, 115, 116, 122, 129, 131
Newton, Isaac, 69
Nixon, Richard, 42
Northeastern University, 4, 37, 40
NWA (Niggaz With Attitude), 41

Oberholzer, Felix, 54
OED (Oxford English Dictionary), 68–70
Oliver, Kenneth, 132
open source software, 9

Parody Doctrine, 123
Patel, Marilyn Hall, 56–57, 67
pathos, 7, 54
Patterson, Lyman Ray, 45–49
PDF (Portable Document Format), 143–46
Peel, John, 87
peer-to-peer, Napster as model 3–5, 43–44; post-Napster

popularity 6; debates over 6–8,12, 20–21, 51, 76, 83, 100, 107, 114–17, 120–21, 126, 143, 146; use by colleges 14, 19, 145; putative impact on record sales 54; users portrayed as thieves, 60; efficiency of 64–65, 77, 86; dependence upon "shared folders" 92–93, 98–99; downloads of motion pictures, 105; potential of, 126, 127, 141, 143,145–48 ; as foundational to Internet, 128–29

permission requests, 15, 24, 42–43, 55, 61, 69, 82–83, 100–4, 143, 147, 149, 150

Perry, Lee "Scratch," 124

photocopier, 140

Pierre-Louis, Stanley, 92

piracy, in Ukraine 9–11, VCR as tool for 57; shifts in meaning 67–84

Pirates of the Caribbean, 71, 73, 76

plagiarism, 131

player piano, 129

Pop, Iggy, 10–11

Porter, James E., 20, 130

Presley, Elvis, 42

public domain, 8, 100–3, 126, 147

public policy, 7, 43, 61, 108

R.E.M., 10

Rader (Slashdot pseudonym), 112–13, 117

Rakoff, Jed, 81

record industry, 11, 39, 116–18

record labels, 3, 4, 11, 35, 90, 112

reel-to-reel tape, 117

Rehnquist, William, 139

Rhapsody, 122, 135

Rhetoric Review, 130, 156

rhetorical theory, 7, 38, 107–8, 120–21

RIAA (Recording Industry Association of America): suit against Napster 6, 34; lawsuit campaign against users of peer-to-peer networks by, 6, 86–93, 97, 99, 121; use of hyperbole, 52–56, 66, 68, 77–82; positioned as tyrant 110; price-fixing 112; uploading of bogus fules 119; arguments against copying music onto computers, 134–35; participation in Grokster case,136

Richardson, Eileen, 40

Ritter, Jordan, 33

Robertson, Michael, 77–83

Robin Hood, 106

Rosen, Hilary, 79, 82

Ross, Andrew, 31–32, 35, 44

Rothstein, Edward, 116

Royster, Jacqueline Jones, 20

Scalia, Antonin, 137

SDS (Students for a Democratic Society): Port Huron Statement, 27

Seabiscuit: variable prices of editions across media 72–76

Secor, Marie, 120

Segaller, Stephen, 26–28

Selfe, Cindy, 130

September 11, 2001 terrorist attacks, 105

SETI (Search for ExtraTerrestrial Intelligence), 147–48

Sharman BV, 136

Slashdot, 112–14

Sonny Bono Copyright Term Extension Act of 1999, 101, 129, 141

Sony, 57, 108, 122, 133, 137-39

Sony v. Universal Studios, 57-8, staple article of commerce doctrine, 133–40

Souter, David, 137–40
Soviet Union, 115–18
Spider-Man, 18
spyware, 12
Stallman, Richard, 28, 39, 83, 84; Free Software, 28; GNU, 28; GPL (general public license), 28
Stapp, Scott, 53
stasis theory, 107, 120–21
steganography, 70
Stevens, Cat, 104
Stevens, John Paul, 133
Stevenson, Adlai, 116
Stooges, The, 10
Streamcast, 131, 136–40
Strumpf, Koleman, 54
students, 4, 14–20, 51, 131, 141, 145–46
Sullivan, Lorraine, 93–96

TEACH Act, 16–19, 141
Thomas, Clarence, 137
Thomas, Douglas: *Hacker Culture*, 23
Time (magazine), 34, 38, 52
Tucker, Carlton, 23

U.S. Constitution, 14, 46, 78; First Amendment, 149
U.S. patent law, 48, 69, 75, 78, 119, 133
U.S. Supreme Court, 55–58, 78, 128, 131–36, 140
Ukraine, 8–11
Ulrich, Lars, 42, 43, 53–56, 60, 116. See also Metallica
University of Minnesota, 149
University of Texas's "Copyright Crash Course," 16
UNIX, 28

USA Today, 117
Usenet, 60, 128

Vaidhyanathan, Siva, 20, 60; *Copyrights and Copywrongs*, 127–28; *The Anarchist in the Library*, 64
Valenti, Jack, 105–7; Boston strangler analogy, 107
Variety, 73
VCR (Video Cassette Recorder), 57–58, 107, 129, 134–38
Viant, 106
videotape, 57–58, 73, 134
Vietnam, 106, 112–14
vinyl, 59, 65, 117
w00w00 (Internet Relay Chat channel frequented by hackers), 32–33

Wah (Slashdot pseudonym), 113
Wainwright, Loudon III, 86–88
Warner Music Group, 93, 108, 119, 122
WELL (Whole Earth 'Lectronic Link), 28–29, 39
West, Susan, 130
Wilco, 102–3
Wilson, Stephen V., 136
Windows (operating system), 9, 12
WIPO (World Intellectual Property Organization), 47
Wired, 78, 154
Woodmansee, Martha, 20, 130
World Wide Web, 4, 128
Written Communication, 145

Yale University Press, 149
Yoos, George, 7

Zikzak (Slashdot pseudonym), 113, 115

www.ingramcontent.com/pod-product-compliance
Lightning Source LLC
Chambersburg PA
CBHW032258150426
43195CB00008BA/500